❧ 1990 ❧
Country Home.
Collection

First Edition. First Printing.
ISSN: 1040-7235
ISBN: 0-696-01879-9

Country Home

Editor: Jean LemMon
Managing Editor: Ann Omvig Manternach
Art Director: Jill M. Carey

Building Editor: Steve Cooper
Home Furnishings Editor: Candace Ord Manroe
Interior Design Editor: Joseph Boehm
Food and Garden Editor: Molly Culbertson
Antiques and Collectibles Editor: Linda Joan Smith
Assistant Art Directors: Sue Mattes, Stan Sams
Associate Features Editor: Beverly Brown
Copy Chief: Mike Maine
Copy Editors: Michelle Sillman, Dave Kurns
Administrative Assistant: Becky Brame
Office Assistant: Jacalyn M. Mason

Contributing Editors
Julie Catalano, Eileen A. Deymier, Sharon Haven,
Ellen Kaye, Bonnie Maharam, Amy Muzzy Malin, Ruth Reiter,
John Riha, Joe Rosson, John B. Thomas, Mary Anne Thomson

Publisher: Terry McIntyre
Vice President/Publishing Director: Adolph Auerbacher
Vice President/Operations: Dean Pieters
Vice President/Editorial Director: Doris Eby
President, Magazine Group: James A. Autry

BETTER HOMES AND GARDENS® BOOKS
Editor: Gerald M. Knox
Art Director: Ernest Shelton
Managing Editor: David A. Kirchner

President, Book Group: Jeramy Lanigan
Vice President, Retail Marketing: Jamie L. Martin
Vice President, Administrative Services: Rick Rundall

MEREDITH CORPORATION OFFICERS
Chairman of the Executive Committee: E. T. Meredith III
Chairman of the Board: Robert A. Burnett
President: Jack D. Rehm

1990 COUNTRY HOME® COLLECTION
Editor: Jean LemMon
Project Manager: Liz Anderson
Graphic Designer: Mary Schlueter Bendgen
Electronic Text Processor: Paula Forest
Contributing Project Editor: Mary Helen Schiltz

Contents

For 10 years, *Country Home* magazine has been bringing you the best in country—architecture, furnishings, decorating, collectibles, and gardening. In 1989—*Country Home*'s 10th anniversary year— the magazine continued that tradition by sharing a variety of new homes along with a sample of lovingly restored old homes. Plus, in a special issue—the Anniversary Extravaganza—the editors revisited select homeowners featured in the magazine during the past 10 years. Now, this second annual *Country Home Collection* combines the best of all those wonderful stories and photographs, so you can rediscover the most memorable homes featured during *Country Home*'s special anniversary year.

February

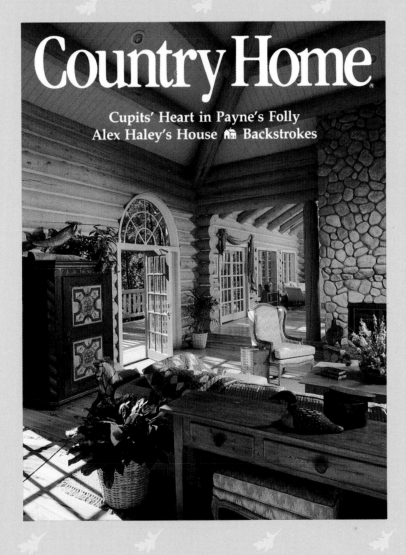

Country Home®

Cupits' Heart in Payne's Folly
Alex Haley's House 🏠 Backstrokes

Cupits' Heart in Payne's Folly

By Candace Ord Manroe
Produced by Eileen Deymier

Bert and Mary Louise Cupit really weren't looking for another home when they found Payne's Folly — and lost their hearts.

John Payne obviously was in love with the place. When his early Georgian dream house was built around 1750 in York County, Pennsylvania, the Quaker Englishman tellingly christened it Payne's Folly.

And folly it was.

While other regional houses were small, Payne's Folly spanned a capacious 2½ stories. It boldly displayed formal Georgian symmetry and style, in contrast to the neighboring architecture which was homespun vernacular. And as if that wasn't folly enough, the home was slickly attired in finely finished stone, not the humble logs that dressed other dwellings in the county.

But despite all that, Payne's Folly kept a surprisingly low profile.

Banked in a hillside, within a foursquare camouflage of firs, it remained demurely hidden from the mainstream eye for the next two centuries. Only cornfields hemmed its original 200 acres, and not a single house neighbored the lonely, unpaved road leading to its door.

Before owners Bert and Mary Louise Cupit purchased the property 15 years ago, it had stood vacant 40 years. Its previous owners had been transferred out of the area before moving into the house—but only reluctantly agreed to sell, hoping someday to occupy the home.

For Payne's Folly, all this had one propitious effect: Time didn't just tread lightly, wielding

Opposite: Payne's Folly was a sophisticated anomaly when built in the mid-1700s for Quaker Englishman John Payne. Familiar with the Georgian style, he specified flanking chimneys and a steep gable roof. The house remains incredibly intact. Left: Owners Bert and Mary Louise Cupit returned the home to its rightful historic name after discovering the property cited as "Payne's Folly" on an early map.

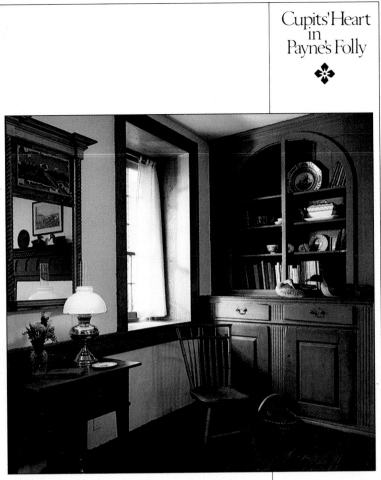

a structural modification here and a decorative change there; it very nearly abandoned march altogether. Little about the original house is changed—not even electricity and plumbing had been added when the Cupits bought it.

Despite groundhogs lodging in the downstairs dirt floor and a January wind shimmying through makeshift plastic window coverings, the first time the couple entered the home they recognized it for what it was: an 18th-century freeze-frame.

A find.

And they made this judgment call, not swept by blind emotion, but with calculated thought. Owners of Cupit Antiques, they are long-time collectors and dealers of country Pennsylvania—"long before we even dreamed of owning that kind of home," says Mary Louise. In addition, Bert is both a furniture and house restorer, a craftsman. When the couple spotted Payne's Folly while meandering down back roads on business, then, they fully grasped its implications.

"Poison ivy and brambles were growing up all over it, the door had fallen in, and little varmints had moved in—it looked spooky—but we didn't see any of that. We only saw the good things," says Mary Louise.

Left: *The parlor's Jacobean mantel is again blue, as when built. Pennsylvania-Dutch antiques complement the built-in chimney cupboard.* Above: *The parlor's Dutch cupboard and woodwork are perfectly preserved.* Below: *Local salt-glazed stoneware foots the original stairs.*

"It was straight. Quite restorable. Nobody had vandalized it. Ninety percent of its original features were untouched. Bert had the trained eye to know it would be a gem."

He recognized that, here, time seems to have been tamed, giving sway to early features too distinctive to easily melt into the mindless motion of the calendar. The original ocher paint is pristinely preserved; huge slate hearthstones still flank the 10-foot-wide kitchen fireplace; the old tongue-and-groove paneling retains its gracefully beaded edge.

The chestnut, oak, and wide-plank pine floors, some boards still bearing the original numeral markings, were "in such good condition upstairs we didn't have to replace a single board," says Mary Louise.

After buying the property—by now reduced from 200 to 2½ acres, the Cupits did not define their challenge in terms of what to do to the old structure; rather, in what not to do. "We wanted to do very, very little to make it lose its authentic flavor," says Mary Louise.

Just as a good story can best tell itself, succinctly, without the resistance from too much authorial puff, so could their house make its strongest statement unimpeded by them. The house is that good, the Cupits reasoned.

Restraint was their decorating mandate. With their favorite early Pennsylvania pieces,

Left: *The kitchen/keeping room's 10-foot fireplace retains its original slate hearthstones. The beamed ceiling is original.* Above: *Ely, the family cat, naps in the kitchen's old milk wagon.* Below: *The 200-year-old door handle has a hand-hammered thumb latch applied with rosehead nails.*

11

the Cupits created tightly edited rooms that grant architectural elements their full due.

Structurally, they employed a similar philosophy. A new roof was essential and, to be habitable, the house required electricity and plumbing. The exterior stones were repointed, and the dirt floor downstairs was covered with brick pavers.

But beyond those essentials, nearly all else was left alone, including the floor plan. The Cupits put all rooms except one to their original use: The old cooling room now functions as a modern kitchen. Meals, however, still are taken in the adjoining original kitchen, or keeping room, with its enormous fireplace that stays lit winter long.

In allowing the house to speak for itself, and in fleshing out its history through research aided by Lynn Rozental of Vermont, the Cupits brought Payne's Folly from obscurity into recognition: It was a shoo-in for listing on the prestigious National Register of Historic Places.

The house originally conceived as one man's folly once again is commanding notice. And like their home, the Cupits also have gone full circle: After a 40-year marriage that began in an early stone house and evolved into newer homes, they are rediscovering the joys of a rock house rife with history—this time, with grandchildren to share in the fun. □

Opposite: The bedroom desk is Pennsylvania pine with original paint and hardware. The hand-hewn chestnut beams are original. Above: *This bedroom's paint trim is the original ocher.* Below: *Apt antiques include a sunburst quilt and pull toy.*

Backstrokes

 Faux finishes take a Kansas City high rise back in time.

By Candace Ord Manroe
Produced by Mary Anne Thomson

An azure sky, still and flat as the canvas, is first to play trickery in the room. Flooding through the window, it masquerades as part of the interior—a great chunk of blue seemingly shellacked within the frame, as indelible as any other appointment.

Left: *Faux-finish and real foliage merge around a Victorian aquarium in Bruce Burstert's* *garden room. Above the terrarium are a circa-1860 tole planter and four 18th-century bird prints.*

Photographs: William N. Hopkins

15

☐ Backstrokes ☐

Of course it isn't. The sky is real. In a matter of hours it will wear cave colors, not this rich shade of happy midday. But such attention to reality is hardly the point here. This is the Kansas City, Missouri, apartment of Bruce Burstert and Robert Smith, a rare respite of a place where illusion, fancy, and bold imagination aren't outlawed but are encouraged and nurtured. A place where reality isn't fixed but, every now and then, takes a wild twirl with whimsy.

As co-owners of a shop called Robert Raymond Smith Oriental Rugs, Bruce Burstert Decorative Arts, Bruce and Robert determined that the reality they wanted to create for their apartment is a blend of Robert's favorite rugs and textiles with Bruce's antique European and American furnishings from the 18th, 19th, and 20th centuries. The result is eclectic—and effective. A fresh twist to the notion of country.

Bruce, as an interior decorator with considerable talents as a faux-finish artist, wanted his personal

Above: *Bruce Burstert, left, has created an unlikely haven of European country in the Kansas City, Missouri, high rise he shares with Robert Raymond Smith and their dogs, Charles and Ricky.* Left: *Hitchcock chairs flank the living room's reproduction French baker's table designed by Bruce. An antique Missouri wardrobe and Turkish Ushak rug meld well.* Right: *Bruce's mural graces the entry.*

☐ Backstrokes ☐

Left: *Old-world charm abounds in the faux-marble living room. An Ionic capital, circa 1840, pulls together an American arts and crafts leather chair and a smaller Biedermeier chestnut and leather chair. Twill curtains soften the architecture of the Federal fanlight and the circa-1800 Massachusetts dressing table, still in its original white paint. Above: Bruce created architecture by painting cornices faux marble. Right: His painted baseboards and trompe l'oeil walls create an old-world ambience, playfully imaginative.*

interior to be painted the shades of old Europe, a country retreat as venerable and mellow and sparkling as a Tuscan villa—or the wine you might drink while there.

That's exactly what he did. Every paint-crackled molding and faux-marble cornice appears besotted with antiquity; the trompe l'oeil walls and ceilings smack of a vintage European country home; a naive 19th-century-style mural declares a certain timelessness. At the deft strokes of Bruce's brush, streams of traffic jockeying for lane space outside the sixth-floor apartment are forgotten; the midtown neighborhood teeming with pedestrians, cyclists, and apple-pie Americans out walking the dog simply disappears.

Bruce's interest in faux finishes emanated from his regard for painted furniture. "I became interested first in painted furniture—how the finishes were done—and did my own research and experimentation. From there, I realized that almost anything looks better against the warm environment that can be created with paint.

Here, I was trying to provide that kind of environment," says Bruce.

"The paint becomes the architecture, the bones. I thought out the finishes, room to room, as all going together as one total environment.

"The main reason it works is because I like all of the pieces in the apartment," he says. "The second reason is the color. The key to putting diverse, unrelated furniture together really is one of color and form, rather than period or style. This apartment has the architecture to be a Federal room, but if it were totally furnished in 1810 antiques, it would bore me. I don't like rooms that are decorated in one style."

In the living room, this philosophy translates as a Biedermeier chair sharing space with a circa-1800 Massachusetts dressing table in its original white paint, and as an American Hepplewhite sofa bathed in soft light from lamps both designed and painted by Bruce.

And under the banner of old-world country, all the

Right: Bruce marbleized the garden room's built-in cupboard, imbuing it with antiquity. Yellowware, red lacquer, and tole accent the yellow-glazed walls. A garden chair and marble-top table create a balcony effect with the thriving topiaries in the window. A French tole wall planter and a pedestal-based Victorian aquarium turned terrarium stand nearby. Left: Bruce's checkerboard paint over asphalt tiles creates a vintage kitchen look. Top: Cupboard drawers outlined in gray and white create a 19th-century painterly effect.

Backstrokes

diversity is unified through Bruce's architectural paintwork. As is only appropriate for something so inventive, his faux finishes don't have a precision look. Just the opposite.

"I like things to be underdone," says Bruce, who only lightly prepared the walls, deliberately leaving some existing cracks in the plaster before applying paint.

"In this apartment, I preferred working with the imperfections. They provided the texture that only time can give, impossible to achieve on smooth, new drywall. I could be more precise but it would lose its excitement. I want things done very simply, a little rougher, so there's still room for imagination. There's too little of it left in the world."

Bruce and Robert's apartment is one small holdout where that particular paucity isn't a problem; where imagination still dances happily and with abandon across walls and windowsills—full of possibility, like the faraway azure sky.□

Right: *Bruce's bedroom ceiling is a cloudy blue with crescent moon; walls are yellow-washed with faux panels. Old linen sheets link mismatched windows; the Biedermeier bed wears new ticking.* Left: *German homespun decorates the American rope bed in Robert's room. A Kurdish saddle cover on the wall and Mondrian-copy rug show his affinity for textiles.* Above: *A European relic spells Old World.*

Alex Haley's
HOUSE CALLED
Annie

By Joe Rosson with Ann Omvig Manternach

Top: *Pulitzer-prizewinning author Alex Haley surveys his renovated 1800s farmhouse located 15 miles north of Knoxville, Tennessee. The house had been abandoned for* at least 30 years when the author of Roots *first saw it.*
Above: *The peace and security the house offers inspired Alex's wife, My, to call it "Annie."*

Photographs: William N. Hopkins, Hopkins Associates.

Left: *As the walls in the living room attest, green is Alex's favorite color (no blue was allowed in the house). The room is dominated by an apothecary cabinet that was made in Knoxville, Tennessee, in the 1870s and today is used to display some of Alex's awards. Even though the piece is solid walnut, the maker painted the grain to look like oak.*
Below: *Alex's wife, My (short for Myron), is partial to the screened porch just off the kitchen/keeping room. Not only is it a good place to curl up with a book, the fresh air makes it this health addict's favorite place to exercise.*

When Alex Haley, author of *Roots*, traveled to East Tennessee to speak at the 1982 World's Fair, he had never owned a house. Little did the Pulitzer-prize winning writer know that the area's people and its past—as well as its homes—would lay claim to his sensitive historian's heart. Today, nearly seven years later, Alex owns several houses in and around Knoxville and resides in each as the mood strikes or the occasion arises.

Not bad for a man who once took inventory of his possessions only to find that the sum of his assets amounted to a typewriter, a desk constructed of sawhorses and a door, two cans of sardines, and 18 cents. The coins and cans he saved, and after the success of *Roots* had them framed. Never one to take life's rewards for granted, Alex keeps this memento as a reminder that, "If you really want to do something, you have to hang in there in the tight days or it will never happen."

Alex's life centers on work; where he works is where he lives. Two to four months of the year home is a freighter at sea, but the rest of the time it's a recently acquired English-style house in the city, a condo near the airport that he uses when he has early flights, or his special place, the farm.

"I use this house for impulse," Alex says of his rural refuge located 15 miles north of Knoxville. "This is one of the treats to myself. I could care less about a limousine—that wouldn't interest me. But I really enjoy having residences, a few, and that's a blessing because most people have [only] one."

The farm, with its T-shaped, tin-roofed house, lies sheltered in a verdant bowl of land. There's a pond and gazebo, old barn, acres of timber and farm fields, and a stream spanned by a swinging bridge. Three guest cottages are tucked in the trees beyond a split-rail fence. A retreat for all who venture here, little of the outside world intrudes the Haley domain. No noise, no lights, no neighbors within view.

"If I feel like it, I can come out here and work at the table in the kitchen or go over to one of the guest houses and sit out on the screened-in porch," he says. "It's nice to be able to go whenever your impulse says, 'Why don't you go do that?' And you go do that."

It's not a surprising attitude for a man who describes himself as having been a lifelong gypsy. Born in Ithaca, New York, in 1921, Alex was reared along with two younger brothers in Henning, Tennessee. After finishing high school at 15 and a short stint in college, where he decided books were not for him, Alex enlisted as a messboy in the U.S. Coast Guard. During the 20 years he followed the sea, urgings (and attempts) to write followed him.

In 1959 he retired as the Coast Guard's first chief journalist and turned to free-lance magazine writing before publishing his first book, *The Autobiography of Malcom X*, in 1965.

For Alex, one book led to another. Haunted by his grandmother's vivid tales of family told during his childhood days back in Henning, Alex set off on a journey across 200 years and six generations in search of a man she had called "the African." Ten years, half a million miles of travel, and many cans of sardines later, the Haley family tree—*Roots*—was complete.

The sense of people and place and

Annie

Below: *Dinner at the farm is often served outdoors, but when small groups do gather in the dining room, they are seated around the circa-1830 cherry banquet table from Kentucky. The Greene County, Tennessee, sideboard is made from seven different woods. It, too, was made in the 1830s.*

Right: *The dining room was in sad shape before the renovation began.*

Before photographs: Courtesy Donna Kendrick

Left: *Many pages of manuscript have been written on the kitchen's Victorian worktable. The cabinets are a dusty barn red and, as Alex says, "It looks like Grandma's kitchen with a microwave."* Below (from left): *Farm manager Richard Yeary, household manager Jan Hayes, and the guard at the gate, Mark Whaley, are the glue that holds the place together, according to Alex.*

time Alex discovered during his search is, perhaps, the impetus for his current status of homeowner. For him there's a new appreciation of belonging, of coming home—be it to one house or several. Intrinsic to this belonging is the assimilation of the heritage that even a simple country house offers.

Alex's description of the farm and the financial status of the family who lived there is a case in point. "The main house was begun in the 1830s as a small cabin with one large room downstairs and two small rooms upstairs," he explains. "In the 1870s, as the family became more prosperous, the front part of the house was added to the original structure in a manner usually called crossing the T."

"This is a house that begs to be touched," says his wife, My. "Walls invite you to touch them, and the floors have a kind of organic smooth feel that says that the wood has been here longer than our combined lifetimes."

Although My spends much of her

time in Los Angeles where she runs a company that specializes in natural-food cookies, she feels the influence of the house so strongly that she has named it Annie. "I was thinking the other morning when I woke up that if I were to give the house a name it would be called Annie . . . Annie feels old and stable and peaceful."

This was not always the case. When Alex first saw the house, it had been unoccupied for at least 30 years. There was no bathroom, no kitchen, no plumbing, no electricity. The floor in the oldest part of the house was rotten, the fireplaces had collapsed internally, and animals used the place for a refuge. Although restoring the house was not cost-effective, Alex never considered tearing it down.

Instead, he found a can-do renovator named Donna Kendrick, and together they began a project that eventually cost well into six figures.

Donna will never forget the night that Alex introduced her to a crowd at

the nearby Museum of Appalachia as the renovator of his newly acquired farmhouse. "I swear to you," she recalls, "everybody in that room looked at us as though we were totally insane. They all thought we were crazy, and as a matter of fact, at the time, so did I.

"But that was before I knew Alex," she continues, "and understood that a sense of history and of people living, loving, and dying in a place meant more to him than the place itself."

During the renovation, Alex's affinity for the past was contagious. "When the carpenters took up the flooring in the kitchen," Donna says, "they found original 1830s hand-hewn timbers under the floorboards. Several were rotted away and had to be replaced."

As the crew began installing newly milled pieces, the appearance of the smooth, machine-cut supports seemed out of place. "So on their own they got in there with an ax and worked on the new timbers until they looked like the old ones. Even though no one would

Below: *The keeping room, with its pine walls and fieldstone fireplace, is the center of life in the Haley farmhouse. When the house was renovated, the 1830s mud-mortared fireplace was inoperable and had to be taken down and rebuilt.*
Right: *Prior to renovation, the board walls of the room were painted. The door to the porch was replaced with French doors to allow light to fill the room.*

ever see their work, they just had to do again what had been done before."

Donna's concept for renovating the house was to make it look like 10 generations of the same family had continuously lived there, changing the house and its contents over the years.

"In doing this house we kept what we could, all that would work, and I think we kept the essence of everything that was here. I also think the changes we made were changes that a family might have made as time went on. There is an eclectic mix of old and new that is appropriate for the one hundred and fifty years this house has been here. In a way, I feel the house did not change so much as it just grew up," she explains.

With the work complete, Alex feels most at home in the kitchen/keeping room located in the oldest part of the structure. "This kitchen seems to symbolize how I feel about this house," Alex says. "I was a [ship's] cook for six years in the Coast Guard. That's where I started writing, and I have written a great deal right here on this kitchen table."

Time seems to take a rest in the Haley house, then makes running leaps to the present. "The fireplace at the other end of the room was built in the 1830s," he muses. "When I'm in here I think how many fires it has held, how many meals it has cooked. Then I glance from the fireplace to the microwave and it's kind of awesome."

The Haleys use the farm extensively for entertainment. It is not unusual to find every spare room filled with friends from the publishing and movie industries. It also is not unusual to find the grounds filled with a few hundred people eating fried catfish, riding wagons over farm lanes, or listening to music played from the gazebo.

"When this place was fixed, I wanted to share it with friends," he explains. "The people who come here respond so warmly and beautifully that it really is a joy to have them. Big-city people are not generally exposed to this kind of country atmosphere."

There's a solace for many in the simple things that the farm offers. "What seems to fascinate them the most is the morning mist coming up off the water and the fish jumping," continues the writer-turned-host. "They may see a rabbit or a squirrel, and the ducks will be over begging. In most cases that sets the tone for their stay."

After being greeted by Alex's throaty "Hi, Buddy," and firm handshake or hug, guests soon meet farm manager Richard Yeary, guard Mark Whaley, and Jan Hayes, who arranges the Haley household affairs. Most are quick to realize that these people are not so much employees as members of the family. A warm mutual admiration society exists between Haley and the people who help organize his life, and this bond of friendship adds significantly to the cozy aura that surrounds the farm like a motherly embrace.

That embrace seems to envelope all who share the farm. "I feel that this house is like an elder in the community," says My. "I think that Annie is blessing the work that goes on here, and that she gives us welcome. The house feels feminine; you can't come in here without a sense of her arms reaching out. . . . When I go to sleep at night, there is a feeling that the house breathes with me, that there is a kind of womblike protection that gives me comfort and sustenance." □

Annie

Below: *Located just a step away from the study, Alex's bedroom is dominated by a pair of turn-of-the-century four-posters with mushroom-shaped headboards.*

Right: *From the beginning, renovator Donna Kendrick had doubts about the Haley project. "Logically and realistically, I thought I was going to have to tell Alex that the house was too far gone to be saved economically, and that in terms of pure architectural interest and pure restoration capabilities there was no reason to save it." Then she realized that Alex's passion for the sense of history, of people living and dying there, meant more than the structure itself. Annie was saved.*

April

Country Home

Très Magnifique 🌳 Bear Basics
Homespun Harmony in the Texas Hill Country

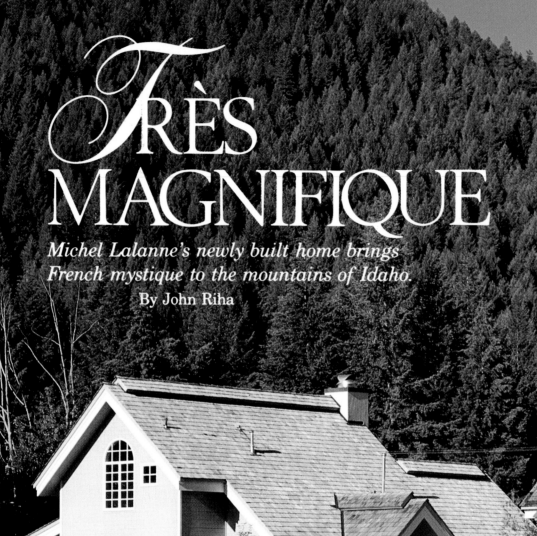

TRÈS MAGNIFIQUE

Michel Lalanne's newly built home brings
French mystique to the mountains of Idaho.

By John Riha

Left: *The home of Idaho antiques dealer Michel Lalanne snuggles up to the Sawtooth Mountain foothills near the town of Ketchum. Plenty of east-facing windows capture the strong morning light in every season.*

Top: *Michel takes a restful moment near one of his carefully tended wildflower gardens.*

Above: *A detail of the front door shows the simplicity and grace of modern cottage architecture.*

*W*arm Springs Creek spills down the Sawtooth Mountain Range just west of Ketchum, Idaho, and tumbles over granite rocks and boulders worn smooth from a thousand years of gentle washing. Although Ketchum is but a snowball's throw from Sun Valley ski resorts, its full-time residents are keenly attuned to the year-round beauty of their surroundings. Often, their appreciation is reflected in the homes they build.

Case in point is the house of antiques dealer Michel Lalanne. Nestled near the friendly murmurings of Warm Springs Creek, Michel's home is a hybrid of European cottage architecture and New England sensibility. With the thickly timbered ridges of the Sawtooths as a backdrop, Michel's house offers fresh, unpretentious simplicity and perfect proportion, all set against the vast landscape.

"I was inspired to build a new house partly because I had this beautiful lot on the river," says Michel. "I was living in an older house, but I decided to create a house that was just the way I wanted a house to be.

Photographs: Tommy Miyasaki, De Gennaro Studios. Architect: Ruscitto/Latham/Blanton

Left: *The cozy living room is brightened by a wall of insulated-glass windows. Nine-foot ceilings, distressed beams, and a small fireplace add old-world charm.*

Top: *The air-lock entry features a set of antique glass passage doors. Windows in the entry offer a view of a sun-filled breakfast nook awash with morning light.*

Above: *All drywall features rounded corners and hand texturing to simulate real plaster.*

A big kitchen because I love to cook and a nice yard because I love to garden. It is close to my shop and it suffices my needs."

Working with the Sun Valley architectural firm of Ruscitto/Latham/Blanton, Michel devised a smaller home custom tailored to his life-style. Of primary importance was the large kitchen and attached dining area that would allow him to converse and sip wine with his guests while he prepared one of his fabulous meals. Although there is a fireplace in the cozy living room, there is another one positioned in the dining area for warmth and ambience. Not surprisingly, this dining area fireplace is double-sided and also services the patio. There, in the heat of the summer, Michel can grill in the company of good friends as Warm Springs Creek surges past his backyard.

"The house is really geared around Michel's expertise in cooking and entertaining," says Jim Ruscitto. "It was important that his house incorporate this aspect of his life."

Another feature that was important to him was a little morning breakfast room on the east side of the house where he could

TRÈS MAGNIFIQUE

Opposite: *Michel's kitchen forms the heart and soul of his home. Designed for cooking as well as entertaining, the kitchen includes a dining area. Choice European antiques lend warmth.*

Above left: *The comfortable dining area nestles at one end of the kitchen. The wide windows overlook Warm Springs Creek.*

Above right: *Michel's collection of antique pots and pans accents the kitchen.*

enjoy morning coffee and mull over books on antique furniture.

"We didn't have a motif we were trying to copy," says Jim, "but the way we described it from the beginning was a cottage. So we wanted to keep the overall scale down to 'cottage' proportions, and we made the roofline steep and used dormers. The main house is about eighteen hundred square feet."

The entire house is a reflection of Michel's personality. The second level, for example, is devoted to the master bedroom and bathroom.

"I cherish my privacy in life," says Michel. "That's why I wanted to have the whole upstairs to myself. I also respect other people's privacy, which is why the guest bedroom in the main house has its own patio and entry doors."

Michel's many fine European antiques would also influence the architectural design. As a boy in Paris, Michel grew up in a house filled with wonderful old furniture. Although he came to the United States as a ski instructor, it would be his appreciation of fine European antiques that would eventually lead him to open a shop in Ketchum. When it came to creating his new

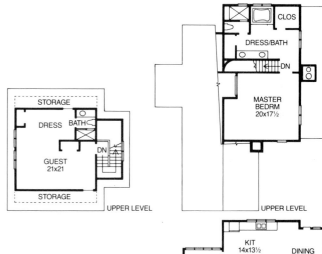

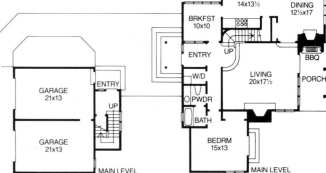

TRÈS MAGNIFIQUE

Left: *High ceilings and larger dormer windows create interesting architectural elements inside the upstairs master bedroom. The visible roofline is characteristic of cottage design.*

Above: *Responding to Michel's request, the architects created a master bath and dressing room dominated by a large circle-top window. Operable casement windows over the tub are a refreshing reminder of European design.*

house, antiques played a major role.

"Michel gave us the dimensions of several pieces of furniture and we would design spaces around them," says Jim. "The dining room table is an example, and in the breakfast room there is an old-fashioned sink that he brought from Europe."

Another factor that had to be considered in the overall design was Idaho's cold climate. Six-inch stud walls and insulating glass windows help thermal performance and prevent heat loss. On the exterior, fiberboard siding stands up well against temperature extremes and also resists deterioration from the increased levels of ultraviolet light found at high altitudes.

"We enjoyed fulfilling Michel's ideas and keeping the house at a reasonable square footage," says Jim. "But, most of all, I like the relationship of the size of the house and garage in terms of human scale. It is one of the most satisfying aspects of Michel's home." □

BEAR BASICS

Handmade teddies are fun-damental to this California country house

By Candace Ord Manroe
Produced by Sharon Haven

No big-city lights could outshine it. For Flore and Neil Emory, an image of the ideal rural life-style was that intense. A neat parcel of countryside laced with trees, pond, and privacy dappled their daydreams with stubborn hope, sustaining them through 17 years of tract-home living while raising four children in suburban Orange County, California.

One day, they knew, resources and reality would answer on their terms, and they would have that country retreat—bestowed with ample elbowroom for doing whatever they wanted.

At the time, they couldn't know all the implications. They couldn't know, for example, that the liberating country life would give birth to bears—handcrafted bears that would make Flore one of the nation's preeminent designers of collectible teddies.

Nor could they know that that business would dictate the decor of their country dream house: a series of styled vignettes, each with its own cache of cuddly bears.

All they knew was the dream: "We had wanted to live in the country all our lives, really," says Flore. When they finally were able to buy their land—an idyllic 4 acres some 70 miles from San Diego in Fallbrook, California— Neil's job posed no problem. He simply opted to open his own custom automobile business (his vocation since 1947) there.

"For a while, we only came out on weekends," says Flore, "but Neil was really antsy to

Right: *Flore and Neil Emory relax at the Fallbrook, California, country dream house they built themselves,* opposite. *(Photograph: Kim Brun Photography)*

Top: *Quaint teddy bears designed and sewn by Flore— one of the nation's leading crafters—spill onto nearly every space of the home, including this wagon in the garden.*

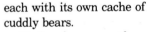
Photographs: Tommy Miyasaki, De Gennaro Associates, except where noted.

41

Above: *Flore's bears share living room space with a circa-1840 American pine hutch displaying a collection of flow-blue china. Other antiques include a Windsor chair, Bliss dollhouse, and hat boxes.*

42

Left: *Flore's firemen bears ride in a reproduction fire wagon on the porch. The bears are clothed in old doll and toy fire hats and buttons Flore has collected for years.*

get out there and build a home. In the same year, we started building our house, put our daughter into college, and Neil started his own [custom automobile] business," she says.

The idea of doing it their way—the feisty independence that ultimately bred Flore's bears—began early on, nearly as soon as the Emorys bought the property.

They immediately launched a do-it-yourself landscaping program,

hand-grading roads with a shovel and spending every weekend for four years getting the grounds abloom.

Knowing they wanted to build the house themselves, they "needed some practice," says Flore, so they warmed up by first constructing outbuildings. From there, a nephew who had just finished his training as an architect got hands-on experience designing the home. He based plans on the couple's dream of a New England-style farmhouse with a

central fireplace.

Except for a little outside aid with wiring and plumbing, the project never left the family: "Our three sons and our daughter, who were college age then, all worked on it. And they brought their friends and boyfriends to

Above: *Flore's favorite sewing spot is by the fire, in an old wing chair covered with a bedspread. The inglenook was designed to accommodate the antique European settle bench.*

Right: *Decoy and bird collections—some made by Flore—decorate her light-filled studio. A European firebench, Texas milk stool, and handcrafted chair add warmth.*

Above: *A "granny's kitchen" adjacent to the stove in the Emorys' real kitchen, left, houses Flore's favorite culinary bears.*

work on it weekends," says Flore.

"It was a circus. It's a wonder anything got built."

The results of the family building project alleviate any doubts that might have surfaced along the way: "We have our own little world," says Flore. "From our property, we can't even see any other homes. This area is all low, rolling hills with ponds and streams—a lot of pilots live around here, because they've seen the terrain from the air and know how beautiful it is."

Their own little world was soon spiced with a stroke of serendipity. One day Flore decided to repair a teddy bear that was among the many antiques she has collected over the years. When she determined that the bear was beyond salvage, she made a new one herself. "I liked it, so I decided to make five of them as Christmas gifts for our younger grandchildren— the ones I thought to still be the right age for teddy bears. But I sold all five before Christmas. I made five more, and on Christmas Day, the older grandchildren were upset because they all wanted bears, too."

That was 10 years ago. Since then, fans of Flore's bears include not only her grandchildren but hundreds of collectors from all over the country. "My biggest boost was when Linda Mullins wrote her book, *Teddy Bears Past and Present,* and used our home as the setting [for photography]," says Flore.

Opposite: *The dining room, opening onto the kitchen and inglenook, is furnished with an old tavern table and 100-year-old handmade arrow-back chairs with children's names burned into the bottoms.*

Left: *The breakfast nook is an appropriate place for Flore's collection of chickens. She designed and made the two farmer chickens on the bin and the wreath hanging in the window.*

BEAR BASICS

Above: *Flore's bears take a ride in an old prison-made wagon on the lawn. These vignettes abound, continually delighting both owners and guests. Photograph: Kim Brun.*

"And I do her show every year in San Diego."

That exposure has proven more than ample for sustaining a thriving business. Flore devotes long hours keeping collectors stocked in bears. "I work on them every single day because I like to," she says. "I spend anywhere from four to sixteen hours a day working, or, if I'm really excited about it, I'll work until two in the morning. It's something I can do and still watch grandchildren. It's perfect for me."

Before moving to Fallbrook, Flore had never given a thought to sewing teddy bears. "I'd always done something ridiculous, but not bears."

Now she not only has realized the dream of owning a country home, but she has improved on that dream with her bears. The charmingly dressed teddies inevitably find their way into the home and heart—riding in old wagons and goat carts on the lawn, holding school in the living room, or cooking in the "granny's kitchen"

Flore created just for her culinary bears adjacent to the stove in her own kitchen.

"It's just a whole lot of fun," Flore says. "We do exactly what we please and don't worry about whether anybody likes it or not." □

Above: *Old needlework pillows and quilts decorate the upstairs guest sleeping loft. Coal-oil lamps, a Boston potty chair, oak cradle, and circa-1888 sampler add flavor.*

Right: *In a living room corner, Flore's antique schoolroom collection melds with her antique-clothed bears. Such vignettes "help people see how to decorate with bears."*

HOMESPUN HARMONY

★ in the ★

TEXAS

HILL COUNTRY

By Julie Catalano and Linda Joan Smith

Above: *Tim and Carol Bolton's farmhouse, surrounded by fields of bluebonnets—the Texas state flower—rests on 85 wooded acres in the Texas hill country. Originally owned by a German immigrant family who built the house in the early 1900s, the property once boasted a general store and gas station that welcomed visitors and customers from miles around.*

Photographs: Rick Taylor.

TEXAS
HILL COUNTRY

★

Safe at harbor in the Texas hill country, the old farmhouse rides the gentle swells of a bluebonnet sea. As the day wanes, a whisper of wind ruffles the flanking fields of wildflowers like God's breath upon the water, and the house, a sturdy structure of stone and wood, settles down for the night. The windmill creaks, leaves rustle in the evening breeze, and an unseen bird, hidden in a blooming redbud tree, sings softly at last light. Tranquillity and harmony prevail.

It was just such a peaceful setting Tim and Carol Bolton sought when they began hunting for their first home. One day, after months of searching, Tim spotted an ad in an Austin newspaper for a "restored rock home and acreage," and called the owners.

"After talking to them for a while I realized it was out of my price range," he remembers. "But they said come on out anyway. When I saw it I fell in love."

The historic structure that stole Tim's heart was built in 1904 by a German farm family, who later established a general store and filling station on the property. For sale along with the house were 85 acres of the ruggedly beautiful land that characterizes the Texas hill country: land liberally studded with oak, mesquite, pecan, redbud, and peach trees. A wine-making shed, stables, barn, water tank, windmill, and the remnants of that long-ago general store completed the idyllic country setting the Boltons longed for.

Left: *Tim Bolton's collection of antique game boards is the focal point of a downstairs hallway.*
Above: *Knee-deep in a velvety blanket of bluebonnets, Tim and Carol stroll through their rural front yard.*
Right: *A comfortable combination of armchairs and settees is set at an angle in the living room.*

Carol instantly shared Tim's enthusiasm for the property. The best part was the fact that the home's previous owners, who bought the house from the original family, had done all the needed plumbing and electrical work. "We could just come in and supervise the fun part, like taking the plaster off the walls to expose the original stone, and furnishing the house just the way we wanted," Carol says.

Carol describes herself as a "red, white, and blue person," and those bold color preferences are carefully coordinated throughout the house. In the living room a medley of blue and white textiles predominates: a windowpane check on matching wing chairs, a plaid area rug, a ticking stripe on a high-backed settee. Splashes of red—turkey-work pillows and an appliquéd quilt—save the scheme from austerity.

Carol's favorite room is the downstairs sun-room, *left.* "It's like being outside when you're inside," she says. A pair of sofas, upholstered in a contemporary version of homespun fabric, invites lounging, while a few special antiques and folk art pieces—a painted storage box, a piece of original fretwork from the front porch, and a tiny wooden church—give the room character without compromising its comfort.

Left: *Sun streams through large expanses of glass in the downstairs sitting room, which opens onto a garden patio.*
Above: *This wood-and-rock reservoir once stored the water supply and fed it to the main house. Now it's a storage shed, where a welded tin man stands guard.*
Right: *Carol and Tim stripped the walls of their plaster, revealing the roughly cut native rock hidden underneath.*

TEXAS

HILL COUNTRY

★

This mix of new and old characterizes the spirit of the Boltons' home: a lighthearted medley of antiques, collectibles, and contemporary furniture and folk art. In the dining room, for instance, early Texas antiques such as a stenciled corner cupboard from Fredericksburg's Nimitz Hotel mingle comfortably with new Windsor and wing chairs, *right*.

The Boltons weren't novices when it came to furnishing the old house; they own an antiques and home furnishings store, and Tim has been in the business for years. It was a love of fine furniture, in fact, that brought him and Carol together. A few years back Carol's father was exploring the possibility of a furniture business venture and contacted Tim, who had owned a furniture store in San Antonio since he was

Below: *With room to sit at the long center island, the warm and cozy kitchen is a favorite gathering place for guests when Tim and Carol entertain. The island was added, but all of the built-ins are original.* Right: *The corner cupboard in the dining room is an early piece from Fredericksburg's Nimitz Hotel, named for Admiral Chester Nimitz, one of the town's native sons.*

TEXAS

HILL COUNTRY

★

17, for advice. Carol's parents not only began a new business but gained a new son-in-law.

Carol and Tim's current business venture is called Homestead and is on the main street of nearby Fredericksburg. The Boltons' marketing philosophy at the store is straightforward and simple. "We want to reach people who are filling a house that they love with things that they love," says Carol. They are their own perfect customers.

"Our true love was antiques," Carol explains, "and at first that was the backbone of the house. But then, through our business, we became interested in new artists and craftspeople. The marriage of the two here at home came about as a result of what we were doing at the store."

The house itself meshed perfectly with the Boltons' varied tastes. The native-rock walls, roughly cut and warmly colored, provide an old-fashioned setting while a two-story wood-and-glass addition, built by the previous owners, brings the house up to date. The addition houses informal sitting areas both upstairs and downstairs.

Upstairs, the sitting room is part of the master suite and opens to a sleeping area that is wrapped snugly on three sides with the building's original stone walls, *below*. At the far end of the sitting room, *left*, a balcony with an outside stairway leads down to an inviting garden. Carol and Tim furnished their private upstairs space with plump armchairs and a fat sofa, upholstered in a soft blue homespunlike fabric and anchored by a boldly patterned dhurrie rug with an almost southwestern character. Visitors are treated to a stay in another upstairs bedroom, just across the landing from the home's master bedroom suite.

Left: A native rock fireplace lends a warming touch to the wide open spaces of the master bedroom's sitting area. For Tim and Carol, it's a room of their own, featuring folk art pieces made by good friends. Above: A collection of fragile quail eggs is cradled in a miniature egg carton. Right: Tim and Carol's bed is a new piece, handcrafted of Texas loblolly pine.

TEXAS
HILL COUNTRY

★

Left: *A bathroom near the upstairs guest room boasts an antique tin-and-oak bathtub, as well as two prized pieces from Tim's collection of antique game boards and washboards. According to Tim, the washboard, water bleached and knuckle worn, is thought to have been a wedding gift from a groom to his bride.*
Below: *The guest room features a stenciled crib quilt on the wall behind the bed.*

This cozy space with its exposed stone walls masquerades as an old-fashioned nursery, complete with an antique cradle from Pennsylvania, the first piece that Tim and Carol purchased together.

Beyond the stone walls of the old house, the land appears much as it must have more than 80 years ago, when the original owners first made it their home. An herb garden and vegetable garden, nestled among the native rock formations that dot the landscape, are in their early stages, tender leaves growing quickly under the Texas sun. And before long, the peaches the area is famous for will be ripe on the trees and ready for picking.

Carol and Tim can't imagine life anywhere else. □

June

Country Home

Where the
Water Falls
Artistic Endeavors
His & Hers

WHERE THE
Water Falls

A New York fashion consultant's rustic retreat atop an old mill

By Candace Ord Manroe

Vicki Ross pays the price of the New York fashion maven. Night after night, her success is measured by an unrelenting string of business dinners and, day after day, by an ear and index finger sore from a merciless phone.

The apartment she keeps in a Manhattan brownstone—when she's not monitoring the fashion world on jaunts to Europe—reflects her ample good taste and limited time: It's upscale contemporary and requires minimal maintenance. The closest thing to clutter, in fact, is the low pile on Vicki's chic industrial carpet.

That's Vicki Ross of New York.

Vicki Ross of Connecticut is altogether different.

Each weekend, she replaces the race of city traffic for the rush of waterfalls; she forgets the bare-bones design dictates of her urban life and sets about filling every nook of her country cottage with antique finds. And instead of the hard edges of classic Bauhaus, the warm, primitive charm of American rustic furniture holds court in her weekend retreat.

Vicki is first to admit that her two life-styles and homes are a study in opposites: "When I'm in the city, if I'm home, I'm always on the telephone. My life there is very hectic. I leave the apartment at eight

thirty in the morning, come home to change, and then rush out again. My apartment is very controlled modern with absolutely no knickknacks or bric-a-brac. My house in the country is the complete opposite. Decorating it is my therapy. It's better than a shrink, though it's probably more expensive."

About 50 years old, the Connecticut house occupies a mill site from the early 1800s. The waterfalls which fed the mill flank the home, lulling Vicki to sleep at night and confounding friends from the city, who insist that it must be raining. The falls figure heavily into Vicki's attachment to the country place. When friends visit for the first time, she promptly bequeaths them

❦ Top Left: *Vicki Ross leads the fast-paced life-style of a New York fashion consultant during the week.*

Left: *Come weekends, she bids her modern brownstone good-bye and retreats to her Connecticut country cottage situated on an old mill site, atop a waterfall.*

Opposite: *A Ralph Lauren wicker chair is upholstered in Anne Klein blazer fabric in Vicki's living room.*

caps that read, "The House on the Falls." The country house may be at diametric odds with Vicki's city apartment, but the same high energy is at work in both. "In one and a half years, I've tried to collect five bedrooms of furniture—shopping on weekends only," she says.

Vicki buys her antiques in Connecticut, New York, and Massachusetts. Favorites are her collections of rustic furniture, painted pieces, doorstops, and souvenir Indian pincushions.

"In the city, my apartment is monochromatic, with clean surfaces and industrial-carpeted platforms, whereas in the country, there isn't a table that doesn't have a collection of something on it. I try to buy mostly American—really primitive twig and painted furniture. I'm fascinated by twig furniture—how wonderful the contrast is when you take rustic furniture and dress it up with fine linens."

She credits Ralph Lauren for that influence on her personal style. "It's fun to take an old, beat-up farm table and set it with beautiful Lenox and Staffordshire china. Whereas other people might want to use pewter, that contrast is the twist that I like."

The polarity between Vicki's city and country lives isn't so much a reflection of her warring tastes as it is a response to practicalities. "I

Above: *A 19th-century mosaic-painted desk in a bedroom emulates inlay but actually was factory made. Vicki chose black chintz for her wicker rocker. A telling sign of her career is the collection of fashion prints.*

Left: *An old Maine farm table with painted chairs defines the dining room.*
Above left: *A primitive bench with original faded paint and hand-painted Victorian pillow grace what Vicki calls her "feminine" guest room.*
Above right: *Vicki turns consummate collector in the country. Antique doorstops are among her favorite collections.*

WHERE THE
Water Falls

travel to Europe six times a year, and the modern look is easy for me to maintain in the city. But in the country, it's easier for me to have collections. The one problem I have is cobwebs."

Unlike some, Vicki doesn't retreat to her cottage to escape all the trappings of city life; she retreats to fulfill city obligations in the easy country atmosphere.

"It's just a nice environment to do my work in. People think twice about calling you in the country on a weekend. Another thing—you can go to bed at eight thirty. That's kind of normal and you don't have to feel guilty about it."

Further proof that the dichotomy between country and city selves isn't absolute is Vicki's fabric choices for the Connecticut home: In the living room, a 1982 Anne Klein blazer fabric dresses upholstered pieces. "I guess because I'm in the fashion industry, I use a lot of fashion fabrics." Vicki also has used some Ralph Lauren as well as European and antique fabrics.

Although her time in the country isn't idle, Vicki gets the psychological lift she needs to face another New York Monday: "Everyone here's very civilized. It's refreshing to get recharged that way. And sleeping on the waterfalls relaxes me enough to get in my car at the end of the weekend and go back to the city." □

⚜ Above: *An antique Adirondack desk in mint condition was Vicki's first purchase for her rustic furniture collection. Other collections include tramp art (the mirror) and Indian souvenir pincushions.*

⚜ Above left: *Vicki's Adirondack bedroom showcases her collection of rustic furnishings. The new bed was crafted by a Massachusetts artisan. The table is old.*
Above right: *The Ralph Lauren bedroom, so named because of its Ralph Lauren fabrics, is used by Vicki's mother. It features cranberry glass and painted Victorian pillows.*
Right: *Doorstop dogs guard the Adirondack night table; Perry Ellis linens grace the bed.*

BUILDING THE COUNTRY HOUSE

Artistic Endeavors

Modern-day renaissance man
Phil Davison handcrafted his home
near the Oregon coast.

By John Riha

Phil Davison knows that perfection is an elusive goal. As an accomplished artist and an exacting craftsman, he has come to realize that perfection is better defined as a subjective sense of harmony and balance.

"At this stage of my life, I realize that perfection in and of itself doesn't exist," says Phil. "If it does, it's temporary. So I do the best I can do and try not to labor over little details that aren't perfect."

But when Phil does the best he can do, the results often approach perfect harmony. Whether at work in his studio on the dream-soft paintings that are his passionate life's work, or simply laying a path through the extensive gardens surrounding his house, Phil creates with an inherent feel for proportion and graceful design.

And so it is with his home: A snug cottage of less than 1,000 square feet nestled on one-half acre in North Bend, near the Oregon coast. Built entirely

Top: *Phil Davison and his pal, Ginger, take a few moments to enjoy the morning sun and Phil's colorful garden.*

Left: *Inspired by the charming homes of Europe and the solid, rustic barns of Oregon, Phil designed and built this cozy cottage.*

Photographs: Ernest Braun. Floral illustrations: Phil Davison. Floor plan: Carson Ode   65

Near right: *Phil's favorite piece of furniture is this corner cupboard that he found and restored. "I've always been fascinated with old furniture and knickknacks," he says. "As I got older, I began going to local historical museums. By the time I was in high school, I was checking out the junk stores and beginning to collect."*

Below: *A salvaged window offers a lovely view of the garden for anyone using this cozy writing corner.*

by his own hands after a plan he conceived, Phil's home is at once an artist's quiet refuge and a testament to his considerable design skills. Each detail is carefully wrought, and the result is a home that is exquisitely crafted.

"I think almost everyone has a dream of creating their own dwelling," observes Phil. "Perhaps it's wistful thinking, but there's something inherent in our nature. I think maybe there is a little longing there to make your own nest and in an individual style so that it means something to you. Not just a place to park your body."

Phil's house was inspired by wonderful cottages he saw during a trip to Europe, as well as the architecture of the solid, rustic barns that dot the Oregon countryside. Board-and-batten siding and a steeply pitched roof with a jaunty cupola hint at the comfortable, relaxed rooms found inside. Although it is a small home by most standards, Phil finds his house to be scaled with practicality in mind.

"I wanted it to be as small and compact as possible," he says. "Of course, because I was building it myself, I didn't want to tackle a project that would be overwhelming."

Not easily overwhelmed by creative challenges, Phil took heart from his upbringing and the can-do attitude of his family. His father, a shop teacher, schooled him in the basics of construction.

"I come from a family where we always built things," he says. "Everyone had the attitude

Above: *An eclectic mix of pieces furnishes the living room. Phil is especially proud of the proportion and location of the fireplace, one of the elements within the house that illustrates the European cottage inspiration.*

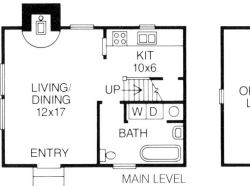

MAIN LEVEL

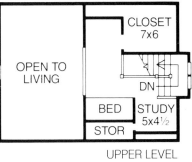

UPPER LEVEL

BUILDING THE COUNTRY HOUSE

Near right: *The no-nonsense plan combines a sleeping nook and office area in the loft that overlooks the living room. A large storage/closet area on the opposite side of the loft (see floor plans on the previous page) provides adequate storage for this compact house.*

Below: *Phil at work in his studio. This airy space is housed in another building that Phil also built on the property.*

that it was not only possible but that all you had to do was *do it.*"

On land near his parents' farm, Phil put his creative intuitions to work. He studied every aspect of the construction process—foundation, framing, plumbing, wiring, even kitchen cabinetmaking—and built his new home with meticulous attention to detail. With an artist's eye for aesthetic light sources, Phil gave his windows special consideration.

"I love old wood windows, and even the best modern reproductions weren't going to do it for me," he says. "Besides, new windows were horrendously expensive. So I took a trip to architectural salvage places in Portland and Salem and made notes of sizes and configurations and eventually bought a selection of old windows."

Building his own home became a logical extension of Phil's creative urges. An accomplished musician, wood carver, gardener, and antiques collector, he views himself as an avid student of life.

"There's definitely a combination of native talent and ingredients that aren't mental in the sense of textbook," observes Phil as he explains his abilities. "I've worked with what I had and educated myself along the way.

"I look around my house and see visual continuity, but it was sort of a seat-of-the-pants kind of process. I just let it happen. My overview was to keep things simple and, with that in mind, I really feel like it's a success." □

Above: *As with almost everything else in the house, Phil constructed the kitchen cabinetry.*

Right: *This vignette represents Phil's interests: he's a classical guitarist, an avid gardener, a collector of Indian artifacts, and he carved the birds.*

69

His & Hers

By John B. Thomas. Produced by Ruth L. Reiter

An Atlanta couple committed eight years to filling their dream house full of history—inside and out.

Cindy and Roger Bregenzer wouldn't curl up and fall asleep on the floor of just any old home. Then again, the 1854 house they uncovered on the outskirts of Atlanta eight years ago offered a comfortable feeling all over—even in its aged floors.

Cindy and Roger had been determined to find an old house worthy of the antiques they had collected with an obsession for three years. When they stumbled across this gem-in-the-rough, they immediately put in their bid and bought the house.

"It was love at first sight," says Cindy. "We knew it was exactly what we wanted so we committed ourselves to restoring it.

"The owners were antiques dealers who had plans to fix it up, but everything needed redoing. It was a mess."

Left: *Nestled amid an ocean of flowers and sheltered by a canopy of elm and maple trees, a stone path meanders up to the front porch of Roger and Cindy Bregenzer's Atlanta home, which was* built in 1854. A landscaping professional, Roger knew the original stone path, steps, and wall were too precious to unearth—his inviting new landscape plan allowed him to incorporate the elements.

Photographs: Rick Taylor

His & Hers

"At the time we were living in a beautiful new house, so our family thought we were nuts. They said to us, 'Where are you going to live?' and we said 'Here.'"

Cindy and Roger had to secure an occupancy permit before moving in the essentials: a mattress, a playpen for baby Adam (their second son, Aaron, arrived a few months later), a refrigerator, and a card table and chairs. The kitchen floor was camp while they reworked the house one room at a time.

"We were never without a project," explains Cindy, who was trained as a mechanical engineer. That's because it took eight years worth of

energy and diligence to renovate a worn-out interior and weathered exterior, redo the landscaping, and later add on and restore an authentic log house.

"I feel in my heart that we couldn't have done it without each other," Cindy says. "We were a team."

"When I felt like giving up," says Roger, "is when Cindy kept me going, reminding me of our pledge to do an authentic restoration."

"We both had our area to concentrate on, and we trusted each other's judgment," says Cindy, who was the general contractor for all the renovation and restoration work. Roger, who owns his

own landscaping business, was in charge of shaping up the 3½ acres outside.

The original house (living room, dining room, master bedroom, kitchen, and two upstairs bedrooms)

Opposite: *Atop an antique Persian rug, an early southern crock overflows with herbs and cuttings. Old stained-glass sidelights help lighten up the heart-pine door.* Above: *In a rare moment, Cindy, Roger, Aaron, and Adam relax between projects.* Left: *In the dining room, a reproduction walnut hunt board with ivory escutcheons hides behind the center section of an 1840s mahogany banquet table.* Below: *In the living room a 1750 maple-and-birch tea table from Windsor, Connecticut, rests on a Persian rug.*

His & Hers

new sense of warmth, Cindy and Roger stripped off piles of aluminum siding and traded them in for handsome 1840s wood siding. "It took several months of searching before we found a house with siding exactly like the original," says Roger.

"We slowly and painstakingly numbered and measured all the pieces of wood, sketched their positions on paper, and kept them in exact order so we wouldn't have nail holes showing all over the place," says Cindy. She then tested dozens of different paints before choosing a cream color for the wood and a rich, dark green for the shutters. "It's the perfect backdrop against the colorful flowers," says Cindy. "It doesn't compete at all."

Old-style black asphalt shingles were used to redo the roof. "We ordered about five times as much as we needed and sorted through each shingle like a deck of cards," says Cindy.

had been victorianized and remodeled by previous owners. Cindy and Roger tried to return most of it to its original splendor.

The majority of the handiwork involved salvaging antiquated material from dilapidated and soon-to-be-demolished homes. "We were often one step ahead of the demolition crew," laughs Cindy.

To give the exterior a

Above: A maple bench, rustic table, and Victorian child's sleigh make the sun porch a classic heartwarming retreat.
Opposite: Next to the fireplace in the breakfast room, a heart-pine grain bin composes a gentle barrier with the dining room. On top is a century-old mahogany spice chest made by Roger's grandfather and an 1800s coffee grinder.
Right: Handcrafted pine cabinets with glass doors make it easy to drape homespun inside; the countertop is solid maple butcher block.

His & Hers

For the interior, Cindy showed the same attention to detail. To grace the kitchen floor with old-fashioned footing, Cindy and Roger drove an hour and a half to Athens to handpick and haul back hundreds of bricks from an old cotton mill. A cutout in the kitchen wall above the sink leads to a sun porch where Cindy and Roger spent nine months cleaning hundreds of chimney bricks dismantled from an 1840 chimney—all in order to make another old-fashioned floor.

The sun porch itself was set up as a transition room leading to a project Cindy carefully planned after the original house was complete. As the boys grew, Cindy realized more space would be needed. An authentic log house, circa 1820, was the perfect solution. Purchased from Hayes Gilliam (a pre-1850 southern-house broker and consultant) after a year-long hunt, the log house was disassembled with the help of a three-story crane, its parts numbered, and then brought back to Atlanta on a logging truck.

With the aid of Lloyd and Jeff Kuykendall, who assisted with the earlier carpentry, four years were spent rebuilding the original four-room structure and adding a guest bedroom on the back of the cabin. The original log house now serves

Above: *Still wearing its early Spanish brown paint, a dated 1848 hunt board in the log house family room is an heirloom from the original owners of the log home. A proud piece of hand-carved Georgia folk art adds to the ambience.* Opposite: *The family room's 100-year-old miniature rocking chair seems even more childlike against the backdrop of a towering 1810 blue corner cabinet from Georgia and rows of hand-hewn timbers.* Right: *Across the room, a second fireplace draws attention to a delicate 1844 spinning wheel.*

as a family room, with two well-worn fireplaces on opposite walls offering plenty of warmth.

Cindy reconstructed the solid-stone firebox chimneys by taking pictures, drawings, and measurements to find the perfect match. When she did, it took eight people, three trucks, a tractor, three trailers, and six weekends to take the chimneys down, number each brick, and haul everything to Atlanta. Then it took months of searching to find a mason willing to even discuss the project. "None of the masons had ever constructed a chimney with solid brick like they used to 100 years ago," says Cindy. "It was a lost art." A year later Cindy finally tracked down two specialized masons from Tennessee. With Cindy by their side, they mixed sand and red clay until the texture and color precisely

matched the old.

"We even used toothbrushes after the masons left at night," says Cindy. "We ate away the wet mortar to duplicate 150 years of aging."

Cindy's determinism assured that everything inside the log house was authentic. Only original materials were used and every detail was systematically set into

Opposite: *Visitors stay in the guest room and cuddle up in a 19th-century handmade pine rope bed covered with a 100-year-old log cabin quilt. A peg rack over the bed holds a child's dress and bonnet.*
Above: *Facing the front porch, the master bedroom shines with bare elegance. A cherry plantation desk and cradle are eye-catching antiques against the soft cream tone of the hand-planed heart-pine ceiling and walls.*
Left: *A mahogany tester bed in the master bedroom is draped in a wool coverlet to ensure extra warmth.*

His & Hers

place, right down to the nails, screws, siding, and locks. Cindy even fitted and reglazed all 141 panes of pre-Civil War hand-blown glass.

"The family room is our favorite room," says Roger. "There's a comfortable feeling in here. It reminds me of how hard people worked one hundred years ago just to survive."

The guest room is located on the back of the log house, a place where a back porch once stood. The couple saved every piece of hand-planed heart-pine paneling from the inside of the cabin and reused them to build the guest room's interior. Even the paint on the ceiling is the original blue. "The room makes people feel good because it re-creates history and reflects stability," says Cindy. Outside the double-hung windows are 3½ acres of pasture and woods.

The picturesque grounds with 4,500 square feet of total garden space, 120 varieties of plants, stone walkways, and low stone walls are the result of Roger's precise planning. He synchronized the layout by making lists of sun/shade requirements, color, height, and blooming time for each variety.

"We wanted a garden that would tie in with the house," says Roger. "A house like this always had an herb garden outside."

Today the house and grounds are so impressive that people constantly drive by for an admiring look, ask for a tour, or leave complimentary notes in the mailbox.

"We like to share with people because we also appreciate a piece of history that's been preserved," says Roger.

As for the future, the two are eyeing a workshop

that doubles as an antiques shop. "I've also been asked to do restorations, so who knows what the future will bring," says Cindy. "But we're certain of one thing—it will be full of adventure and hard work." □

Above: *An old wheelbarrow coated with buttermilk paint carries geraniums, phlox, and asters.*
Left: *The outer perimeter remains for perennials while herbs flourish in four quadrants and the center.*
Below: *Patterned stonework and a grouping of impatiens ensure guests an inviting journey to the front porch.*

August

Country Home

Just a Walk Away

The Other Side
of the Island

Diligence

Just A
Walk Away

Old-world comfort and everyday closeness help this Pennsylvania family keep it all in harmony.

By Ellen Kaye and John B. Thomas

Nestled in a secluded valley bristling with deer and wild geese, a few hundred feet from the French Creek in Chester County, Pennsylvania, Jim and Liz Cherry's home seems as constant as the beech and poplar trees that shroud their 22-acre tract of land.

Hidden from their view, but within shouting distance, a smaller structure houses Jim's mother, Jessie Famous. Both homes are the creation of Jim, a man who enjoys reconditioning 1933 Ford automobiles as much as restoring and

Opposite: In the sitting area of the great-room, a Victorian horse pull toy from Jim's grandmother rides atop an unpainted blanket chest. A narrow painted Pennsylvania corner cupboard fits snugly into a corner next to the stairway. Above: Liz and Jim with daughter Elizabeth outside their home. Left: Embracing the log house on opposite ends are a brick gable housing the fireplace and stairway, and a wood-framed addition containing the master bedroom and bath.

Photographs: Jon Miller, Hedrich-Blessing. Produced with Jill M. Carey

Just A Walk Away

reconstructing 18th-century buildings—his livelihood the last 20 years.

"It started out as a hobby," says Jim. "When we got married I fixed up our first house, and then another, and soon people were calling and asking if I'd do it for them."

Jim had the urge to move farther into the country to build yet another house when he spied this private sanctuary just 45 miles northwest of Philadelphia. "The whole area is under deed restriction so we knew it would be like this forever," says Liz.

The only thing missing was a place to live. Jim was ready to relocate a log house on the property as soon as he could find a quality structure. "I received a call one day from a friend about an Amish farmer's log house," Jim recalls. "I rushed over

there and the farmer was tearing the roof apart, throwing the roof rafters into a huge fire! I pulled the rafters from the fire and persuaded the farmer to sell me the house."

With a crew of seven men, Jim dismantled the 1737 log house within a few days and moved everything onto their new property. Before he reconstructed the house, Jim built a barn, a carriage shed, and a workshop to store his vast collection of tools for repairing old automobiles and old houses.

The log house itself was reconstructed into a great-room—a single space fashioned from the log house's original four first-floor rooms. The entry, kitchen, living area, and dining area are contained in the great-room while a frame addition harbors the master bedroom, sewing

room, bathroom, and back porch. Upstairs are two bedrooms, each with its own dressing room, and another bathroom.

"I love my home," says Liz. "The layout flows so nicely. I don't think there's anything I'd change."

For Jim, change is part of the exhilaration of restoration work. "I'm ready to do another house," he says. "It's like a painting, I guess. When it's done it's done and then it's time to do another. That's been hard on Liz—having to move just when she's gotten things the way she likes them. But she's never complained."

Jim and Liz's two daughters, Jessica, 22, and Elizabeth, 19, don't share in Dad's restlessness. "They don't want us to sell it because it's home," says Liz. "And their friends love it because it's so different."

Just down the lane, Jessie's house is more conventional—with architectural features (like

Opposite: *The great-room's original flooring is random-width tongue-and-groove spruce. Jim added a walk-in cooking fireplace complete with a tiny window for extra light.* Above: *Liz's open kitchen includes Jim's handcrafted cabinets and a pair of up-to-date wall ovens.* Left: *Consistent with the log house, the addition's master bedroom displays beaded ceiling beams and yellow pine flooring.*

Just A Walk Away

a steeply sloped roof) more akin to a Chester County plank house. "It's perfect for her," says Liz.

The size of Jessie's house was predetermined because Jim decided to build it on an old sheep shed foundation he discovered one day while clearing away debris around their stone lane. "I tried to build her something with a lot of character," says Jim. "I wanted something that would fit into the area so I made it look like a tenant worker's house."

Although an original plank house would have been crafted of spruce or pine siding, Jim chose cedar siding for its easy maintenance. The rest of the house is almost a miniature of Jim's: It has a small great-room with a bedroom to one side.

A distinctive feature in the back of the house is a triangle-shaped window which sets off a window seat. "I'm a nature lady," says Jessie. "This window allows me to look at the countryside on either corner of the house. Chester County is known as horse country and sometimes I'll hear the hounds and go to the window and see the hunters ride by in their red coats and black hats."

Opposite: Blue-painted paneling and a triangle-shaped window with window seat add coziness to Jessie's dining/living area. Above right: Jessie enjoys some sun on the back porch. Below: A rear view of the house reveals the stone foundation of its sheep-shed beginnings. Bottom left: The winsome Pennsylvania countryside awaits outside. Bottom right: A corner fireplace in the dining area is classic mid-1700s Chester County English style—decorative and designed for heating, not cooking.

From the back porch Jessie can see even more of the natural beauty that surrounds both houses. "There's a lovely old iron bridge that crosses over the creek," says Jessie. "I call it my bridge."

The charm of the land, however, is secondary to the comfort the whole family shares in being closer to each other. "I can't see her from our house," says Liz. "But I can be down there in a minute. That's what makes it nice. And if either of us needs something, like an egg, we just call the other up and say 'OK, meet me halfway.' " □

THE
Other Side
OF
THE
Island

By Candace Ord Manroe

A 200-Year-Old Long Island Barn
Beckons with Rural Reminders.

At the end of the lane a saltwater
bay laps sanguinely up to the
shoreline. The rhythmic drone of
shallow breakers on the pebble-and-
sand beach is more than nature's
answer to elevator music. Its
constancy is a reminder that in
Remsenburg, New York, past and
present are a continuum, predictable
as the ebb and flow of the tide,
fostering a similar sense of balance
and well-being.

For Long Island preservationists
David and Cristina Kepner, such a
place was the natural starting point
of their search for a historic property
to save. The 200-year-old partially
renovated barn that search finally
produced really came as no great
surprise: wonderful, to be sure,

Opposite: *Built in the late 1700s as a cow
barn for the Tuttle farm in Remsenburg,
New York, this gray-shingled structure has
been renovated as a weekend home.*
Right: *Owners are preservationists David
and Cristina Kepner. David's building
firm did the work.*
Above: *The Kepners chose Remsenburg for
its quiet, rural feel.*

Photographs: Bill Stites. Regional editor: Bonnie Maharam. Designer: Charles Riley, WestPoint Pepperell

but the inevitable conclusion to well laid groundwork that hinged, first, on a careful consideration of locale.

The Kepners appreciated Remsenburg being a part of Long Island's fashionable West Hamptons, while somehow evading the usual trappings of a glamour getaway and the glitterati it attracts.

David, who spent his childhood summers in the Hamptons, immediately recognized Remsenburg's uniqueness: "It attracts a different sort of summer folks—not the jet-setting

Left: *Old brick and the original barn flooring and beams lend authenticity to the living room. New traditional furnishings are upholstered in sheeting for a low-maintenance country French effect.* Below: *An efficient floor plan has kitchen counters separating the living room.* Above: *Tulips in antique Chinese porcelain top an antique table.*

crowd who believe everything they build must be some sort of architectural statement. It's more jeans and boat shoes than cocktail dresses," he explains.

The Kepners discovered a different side of Long Island at Remsenburg—a place of white picket fences where town is a small country post office and the undeveloped vista an heirloom; where a breadbasket history is not relegated to a crusty chapter in the past but retains an immediacy in pace, mood, and the mind-set of the people.

"Remsenburg is a farming community, and it attracts people who don't want to live in glass pyramids," says David. Rather, it is a "wonderful, sleepy little town," adds Cristina.

"It's only in the last few years that New Yorkers have discovered it. It's quieter, friendlier than other places. People are always hiking, running, or riding bikes. The profile of the people who live here is very preservation minded," she says.

With their strong appreciation of history and erstwhile rural ways, the Kepners particularly were charmed by the tangible traces of Remsenburg's agrarian roots—roots that sprang lushly from the silt-rich soil flanking Moriches Bay.

And exemplifying these roots in stellar fashion was the gray-shingled barn that had weathered two centuries of Atlantic "Nor'easterly" storms. One look was sufficient. The Kepners had found their cause.

"Wild pheasants were running across the property," recalls Cristina. "Even though the barn sits on only an acre, there are fields to the front and woods to the side, so that it has the feeling of a lot more land. We fell in love with it."

Built by an early colorful character, Willis Tuttle, the barn features mortise-and-tenon joinery, a building technique largely abandoned after 1830. Tuttle's original clapboard farmhouse still stands near the barn, though the two properties now are individually owned. The Kepners found the notion of barn and house surviving side by side as one more reason to buy and restore the barn.

As a builder, David knew

immediately that a previous—and aborted—renovation of the barn would demand "radical amendment. I walked through and decided to move doors, rearrange walls, enlarge the master bath and kitchen. One of the biggest decisions was to add a guest wing from what had been an old stable, adding a breezeway to connect it to the barn itself. We

Opposite: *A breezeway paved in Vermont stone connects the dining room, in the original barn, to the newer stable bedroom annex.*
Above: *The dining room's French doors open onto a patio and garden; old beams decorate the walls.*
Below: *Vermont slate and custom cabinets create an upscale kitchen.*

The Other Side

ended up creating five bedrooms from the original three," he says.

Restoration entailed a compromise between practicality and purity. "I went to some trouble to recess the drywall to let the support beams and diagonal braces show through, so it would read both as a wall for putting a sofa against and hanging pictures on, and as a barn," David explains.

Steel I beams were buried into cavities wherever possible; elsewhere, they were deliberately exposed, the idea being "some 19th-century farmer finding a sagging beam and shoring it up," says David.

In a concession to the present, a backyard pool was added, but not without one striking allusion to the past: An old corn crib now functions as cabana.

For the interior, the Kepners retained designer Charles Riley. "The barn itself pretty much determined the theme," Riley says.

The Other Side

Left: *The master bedroom, replete with old wood trim, is in the original barn section of the home. A French door in the bathroom (off the bedroom) floods the space with light. The bed and commode are new.* Below: *A perfect reading nook in the master suite is created with a new love seat covered in sheeting that matches the linens and curtains.*

The Other Side

"We wanted colors and patterns for some warmth, but not a lot of expensive fabrics that would be damaged by sunlight and people running in and out from the pool. We used sheeting for upholsteries, bed canopies, and window treatments. They had a lot of wonderful patterns for the country French look we wanted to achieve."

A vintage look but without vintage prices was obtained through new furnishings, whose designs were inspired by antiques. A casual furniture arrangement facilitates the weekend life-style anticipated for the barn.

"The whole point of our buying the barn was to preserve it," says Cristina. "Now we're hoping it can be passed on to someone with an appreciation for its original character." □

Right: *A skylight and soft white walls brighten a bedroom in the smaller annexed structure that was originally the stable. Bed, desk, ottoman, and the overstuffed chair are new; the desk chair is an antique.* Below: *The original barn loft is now a sitting area above the living room. The early barn architecture can be admired from a new wing chair.*

DILIGENCE

By Steve Cooper. Produced by John Riha

"Sweet is the labor, certain
are the gains." This Finnish house-barn
is as solid as an old adage.

Take the old saying above, appreciate its
sturdy truths, understand its practical
wisdom, and apply it. What do you get? Tad
and Marsha Van Valin got a house of ethnic
character and rugged charm. "It's a lot of
work. But the more work we do around here,
the more wonderful it gets," Marsha says.

Photographs: Jim Hedrich, Hedrich-Blessing

DILIGENCE

❧

Today the Van Valin's immense log dwelling rises in Wisconsin's rolling Kettle Morraine hills as testimony to their diligence. From the moment they saw it abandoned 200 miles north of the present homesite, they were struck by its potential.

While exploring Michigan's Upper Peninsula in 1986, the not-yet-married couple found their future home directly in the path of a cut-and-burn timber operation. It was move it or lose it forever. And a serious loss the red pine structure would have been.

"By its sheer size, this is one of the greatest and most unusual of the remaining house-barns in the country," explains William Tishler, a

Detail: *Marsha sells antique samplers like this 1814 Chloe Jenkins design through her business, The Scarlet Letter.* Above: *Felix the cat suns himself near a stairwell.* Right: *The house-barn as it stood in Ishpeming, Michigan.* Far right: *Among the treasures Marsha has purchased at auction is the dark rose-colored semi-antique Lilihan Persian rug. She rescued the portrait, which is dated 1777, from the spider-infested back room of a Cotswold, England, antiques shop.*

DILIGENCE

University of Wisconsin professor, who has surveyed the nation's diminishing supply of old-world house-barns.

The utilitarian design was imported by rural European immigrants in the last century. The name fully defines the 34×48-foot structure. It is both house and barn—sharing common walls front and back. A solid interior wall equally divides human living quarters and what formerly was agricultural storage.

Finnish immigrant Abram Wiipola completed construction of the three-story log house in 1894. Wiipola did some potato farming and hunting as he lived in the house with his wife, Kaisa Katarina; their daughter, Hilda; and sons Emil, Nils, and Otto. Emil, who died at age 83 in 1980, was the last of his family to have residence there.

"Part of the joy of a house like this is knowing its history, but so often you have trouble finding information. We were fortunate that relatives still live in the area who could fill us in. And Emil left a diary," Marsha says.

Among the tidbits gleaned from the diary: Emil shot a deer from his upstairs window on Oct. 7, 1921. The animal was no more than 100 feet away.

"That was the first time I was able to shoot a deer from the window," noted Emil.

Having found a house so rich in history, Tad and Marsha faced the arduous challenge of moving it to their homesite near Sullivan, Wisconsin. Tad, a building restoration professional, brought the skills he has gained moving about 25 log houses during the past eight years.

During the summer of 1986, the Van Valins and friends disassembled the massive home by hand.

"Removing the roof was a major obstacle. We were working pretty high off the ground and it was a mess up there. But once that was done, we just started marking the logs and dropping them down one

Detail: *With hammer, nail, and agility, Tad and his friend, Jim Anfang, raise the roof on a Bohemian log barn outbuilding moved from Kewaunee County, Wisconsin.* Opposite: *Marsha found the three-legged chopping block, which looks like an overgrown milking stool, in a cheese factory. Three-inch-thick countertops were custom-made from planks discovered in an aging bowling alley. Ornate splash tiles came from the Moravian Pottery and Tile Works in Doylestown, Pennsylvania, and are produced today in the same manner they were in 1900. The 1886 stove came from Tad's parents' farmhouse and is still capable of a warm glow. Not shown are nods to convenience—a modern stove and refrigerator. A microwave oven is coyly hidden in a cupboard. Cabinet colors match the original mustard found throughout the house-barn.* Left: *"Elegance" is an elastic term, as the dining room demonstrates. A formal simplicity can be found even in a house-barn with rough timbers crossing an open ceiling. The dining table is an antique, but the chairs came fresh from a shop in Kittery, Maine.*

DILIGENCE

✦

Detail above: *The date carved by immigrant Abram Wiipola in a master bedroom red pine timber marked the completion of the house-barn. Detail* below: *Marsha's sampler collection includes Isabella Fullerton's "Diligence," which hangs in the guest bedroom. The lower sampler is called "Log Cabin" and was designed by Marsha for her business. She is planning another log home stitchery, this one inspired by her reconstructed Sullivan, Wisconsin, dwelling. Right: Marsha spends many of her days creating designs and figuring out how to turn older samplers into kits. Her studio is on the barn side of the barn-house. When she isn't here, she is scouring the United States and Europe for unusual antique samplers. Opposite: One of Marsha's handmade quilts lends a welcoming touch to the guest bedroom. Though the house could easily accommodate more, there are only two bedrooms and both are on the second floor.*

by one with ropes," Tad recalls.

In all there were 441 square logs up to 48 feet long. It took two semi-trucks with loads totaling 32 tons to cart the timbers to Wisconsin.

"How many people can tell you what their home weighs?" asks Marsha.

Disassembling the house-barn took six people 10 days. It took a month to restack, install floors, raise a roof, and add insulation.

Because Wiipola's home was built in a desertlike pocket 70 miles from Lake Superior, only 10 percent

of the logs were lost to decay. Tad also reused pine flooring, window frames, and railings.

"If you consider the amount of work that went into originally choosing, cutting, and preparing those logs, our time was really nothing. There was at least a year of steady work in that building to begin with," Tad says.

The couple took a break for their wedding in the fall of 1986. The honeymoon included a visit to a showroom, where they selected toilets and tubs.

Move-in day arrived in

104

DILIGENCE

Detail: *From the walkway visitors see this plaque honoring the Finnish farmer who built the massive house-barn. Wiipola's neighbors gave the property its nickname, "Smoke Ham," because his sauna frequently doubled as a meat-smoking hut. The dwelling's original shell was probably completed in 1893 and the interior work in 1894. Tad says, "Every time I take a place like this down, I'm amazed at the work that went into it, the craftsmanship. To think it was all done by hand—it really gives you an appreciation for the people who built it." Left: These smaller barns house supplies and Tad's tools. They also shelter the Van Valins' assorted farm animals.*

September 1987, though work is never done. Four smaller log and half-timber barns were reconstructed near the house-barn. Wiipola's sauna was also reconstructed, and Emil's sheet metal stove is fired up for the luxury of weekly sauna baths.

"The sauna is very clean, nicely scented, and bright," Marsha says.

The home itself is surprisingly bright, Marsha having made good use of light from custom windows. Furnishings have come from both New World and Old. Antique chests, samplers, clocks, and rugs create rooms where time is suspended. There is an inviting warmth promising long days lingering over hot cocoa and florid prose.

"Living here is wonderful. It's proven to be even more than we thought it would be," Marsha says.

In keeping with the character of a house-barn, the barn side is still a place of work. It bustles with Marsha's mail-order stitchery business, The Scarlet Letter. She specializes in kits patterned after antique samplers. A favorite is an 1827 sampler, "Diligence," a collection of pithy adages perfectly capturing the yeomanly spirit of the house-barn.

"When we first found this place, our mouths dropped. We knew this was the place. Not everyone would react that way, of course. You kind of put on the blinders and try to see it the way it will be—not the way it is," Marsha says. "And I'll tell you the truth, it's turned out better than I ever saw it in my imagination." □

Country Home.

Déjà Vu

My Kingdom for
A Horse Named
Morgan

Practice Makes
Perfect

"My taste is always changing and softening. I started out with simple country furniture, and I still love that. But I also love chintz, and beautiful color: grays, rose pinks, teal."

—Rosemary Casey

Like a curious trick of perception, Rosemary Casey's home feels oddly familiar. Yet there's also an intriguing novelty here—a vital new spirit that belies the impression of a previous acquaintance. Both sensibilities—the familiarity and the freshness—are equally sound.

Country Home® magazine has visited Rosemary before, in our January/February 1984 issue (pages 53–60). Although she's moved since then, from a 1950s Cape Cod house in New York to a

Déjà Vu

By Linda Joan Smith

Photographs: William Stites. Regional editor: Bonnie Maharam

Above: *We first featured Rosemary Casey's home and shop in 1984. She's put down new roots since then.*

Top left: *A romantic at heart, Rosemary has developed an unpretentious yet elegant decorating style.*

Left center: *A James River colonial by type, Rosemary's classic home actually is brand-new.*

Far left *and* left: *Fine antiques lend richness and substance to each room of the house.*

Design: Rosemary Casey
Builder: John DeCesare

Déjà Vu

newly built James River colonial in Connecticut, her distinctive approach to design has traveled with her. The old look is still discernible—Rosemary loves the simple country furnishings that were her earlier hallmark—but the intervening years have brought a soft new sophistication to her style.

"There are some things I never part with," says Rosemary, whose staples include an elegant highboy, an 18th-century slant-front desk, a colorful painted chest, and a collection of ships' portraits.

Her taste, however, is always moving forward, channeled by a maturing appreciation of the decorative arts as well as the demands of clients and shop customers who call upon her design expertise. "I'm influenced by the cluttered look, and enjoying it more," says Rosemary. "I tend to clutter for a while and then clear everything out, returning to a cleaner look.

"I'm also affected by all the chintz that's available now," she says. The soft floral pattern of chintz in the living room is a major departure from Rosemary's

Right: Shaded in summer by a verdant canopy, the brick-paved patio is an inviting extension of the house and the perfect spot for alfresco entertaining. When her busy schedule allows, Rosemary relaxes here, coddled by flowered cushions in fat wicker armchairs. The mullioned sliding doors in the background lead to the keeping room, where Rosemary does much of her design work.

Above: *Rosemary's original living room featured homespun plaids and quilted pillows.*

Top left: *Subtle stenciling, a painted chair rail, and bull's-eye glass lend a centuries-old feeling to the entryway.*

Far left: *Rosemary's feminine nature has been given full play in the living room, where swags of creamy chintz and slip-covered sofas lend a fresh, romantic air. The ship's model anchored in the corner belongs to friend John DeCesare.*

Déjà Vu

> "I encourage people to collect things—to buy things they really love to give their rooms personality. I can't give them my personality— I have to have theirs."
>
> —Rosemary Casey

earlier style, in which homespun plaids and checks played a central role. The romantic lure of chintz is part of a larger trend she sees in her design work. "People are tired of the starkness," Rosemary says. "They want comfort, and more fabric."

She responds in her own home with upholstered and slip-covered couches and chairs of traditional style, littered with pillows. Soft mohair throws and antique quilts further soften her original bent for austerity.

Throughout the house, small design details express Rosemary's gentle personality without adding undue clutter. Her delicate pink glass plates color the view from a living room window, while hand-painted botanical prints lend a garden's grace to many of the rooms. Early salt-glaze stoneware, rosemary topiaries in green marbled pots, a lacy canopy over her bed—all present subtle facets of her taste. This feminine touch is balanced by masculine items such as a strikingly sculptural ship's model and fine antique decoys

Above: *Rosemary's first store was filled with down-home quilts and checked homespun; her new shop has a softer, romantic look.*

Far left: *A flock of decoys, a cozy fireplace, and a flood of sunlight make the keeping room Rosemary's favorite spot. Authentic details include plastered walls, hand-hewn beams, and a paneled fireplace.*

Left: *In the far side of the keeping room is a bench originally placed in Rosemary's living room.*

Déjà Vu

Above: *Elements from these two settings in our first article have resurfaced in Rosemary's current home.*

Above right: *Mixing antiques and reproductions is Rosemary's forte. In her dining room she surrounded a new Hepplewhite table with a quartet of antique Windsors.*

Far right: *Just off the kitchen and keeping room, this eating area sports sturdy reproduction Windsors with an early pine table.*

114

from the collection of friend John DeCesare. "It unfusses what I do—having a man's things," explains Rosemary.

Along with John's decoys, she blends fine reproductions with her favored antiques and accessories. "I look for classic design," she says. "I want a reproduction of a real Queen Anne leg or a real hunt table—not some made-up thing."

There's no pretense involved; Rosemary enjoys the fact that these pieces are newly made, constructed by craftspeople as skilled as their woodworking ancestors. "I don't like a reproduction that's fakely distressed and all of that. I'd rather it be a straightforward, good reproduc-

tion and not apologize and try to look like an antique," she says.

The house itself provides a fitting backdrop for Rosemary's characteristic blend of new and old. Though the structure is still new, its form has been seasoned by the centuries. Designed by architect Lyndon Eaton and built by John DeCesare (whose passionate attention to detail is clearly evident), the house is fashioned after Colonial Williamsburg's Nicolson House, which dates to the 1750s.

Authentic elements such as nine-over-nine double-hung windows and a gambrel roof with five dormers tether the building to its colonial roots, but modern-

Déjà Vu

"I buy small antiques, like little doll beds and chairs and that sort of thing—I have always been drawn to them. I guess I'll never grow up."

—Rosemary Casey

day construction lifts it to a level that's comfortable and easy to maintain. "I'm enjoying the conveniences of modern bathrooms, closets, and lighting," Rosemary says.

Along with the new house, Rosemary's shop also has flourished. Called "Rosemary," the store has moved from its location in Cross River, New York, (which *Country Home* magazine shared with you in 1984) to its current home in Southport, Connecticut.

Once focused primarily on antiques, Rosemary now fills the store and its annex with fine reproductions, inviting upholstered pieces, and romantic bedding. The canopy bed she sells is her favorite offering. "I'm romantic at heart," she says.

It's that flair for romance, blended with an openness to new design ideas and the solid foundation in the American decorative arts, that has brought Rosemary—both the store and the woman—such stylistic success. Where will it lead her in the decade to come? □

Above: *Sweet country touches and an air of simplicity were the essence of this earlier room.*

Above right: *Old-fashioned elegance reigns in Rosemary's room today: white linens and lace, gleaming silver, gilded enamel.*

Near right: *An old chaise, re-covered in a tiny print and topped with pillows, invites windowside lounging.*

Far right: *A medley of new and old linens, including a tablecloth canopy, wraps Rosemary's bed in romance.*

116

My Kingdom for a Horse
Named Morgan

The traditional traits
of a 200-year-old breed
are preserved on a Vermont farm.

By Candace Ord Manroe

Above: *Richard Haas preserves equine history at GH Morgan Horse Farm, which he owns with Howard Graff.* Below: *Their quintessential New England farmhouse in Townshend, Vermont, is nearly two centuries old.* Right: *A picturesque pond adds to the serenity.*

When the poor Vermont singing teacher bought the small brown stallion in the 18th century, he wasn't asking for much. He only wanted a reliable, strong horse for his personal transportation and the heavy farm tasks of plowing and clearing.

He was not disappointed. Not only was the animal docile and sturdy, it was fast. Justin Morgan raced his horse over many a quarter mile and, legend has it, never lost.

In buying this horse which was to be his namesake, Morgan could not have known he would be establishing a new American breed—the only one to be descended from a single horse. But the

Produced by Linda Joan Smith. Interior photographs: Bill Stites
Outdoor photographs: Linda Joan Smith.

My Kingdom for a Horse

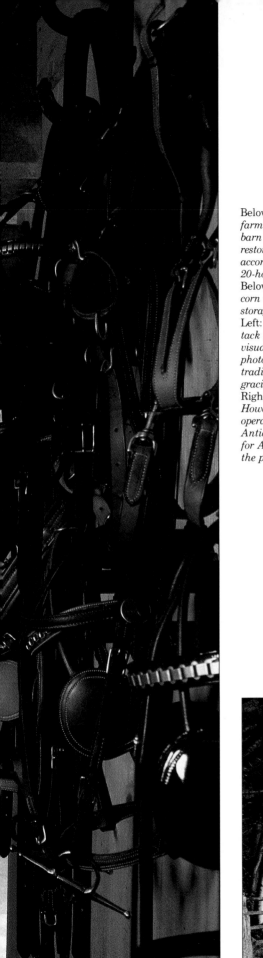

Below right: *The farm's 125-year-old barn was totally restored to accommodate the 20-horse herd.*
Below: *A colorful corn crib is used for storage.*
Left: *The barn's tack room is a visual delight with photographs of the traditional Morgan gracing its walls.*
Right: *Farm owner Howard Graff operates Colt Barn Antiques, a resource for Americana, on the property.*

traits of the small stallion were distinct and dominant.

Thought to be a Thoroughbred and Arabian cross, the animal passed his calm and willing spirit, high-stamina metabolism, and muscular conformation to every foal he sired.

Today the Morgan is a pleasure horse beloved for its versatility in equine events both in harness and under saddle. In Vermont, it is virtually enshrined—as much a part of the state's identity as the Green Mountains, dairy farms, or maple leaves.

When New Yorkers Howard Graff and Richard Haas came to the state 11 years ago visiting friends, they only vaguely were aware that Vermont was Morgan country. That visit was fateful for both the men and the Morgan horse, though.

With no intention of leaving New York City, the two friends found an old farm they couldn't resist, bought it before leaving Vermont, and eventually transformed it into a horse farm dedicated to breeding the traditional Morgan.

Now, during the 200th anniversary of the Morgan, Howard and

My Kingdom for a Horse

Richard have a real stake in preserving a part of America's heritage with their GH Morgan Horse Farm in Townshend, near Brattleboro.

"Most Morgans you see today are show-type Morgans, not the traditional horse. They don't have the original conformation or type or disposition, but have become more like [flashy, temperamental]

saddlebreds," explains Richard, a rider since age 7, who has primary responsibility for the breeding program.

"When we moved here, I discovered the traditional Morgan was disappearing. I didn't like what was going on, and that's how this whole thing started," he says.

Leaving behind his occupation in the computer industry, Richard advertised for the bloodline he wanted and gradually built a herd of 20 horses.

For Howard, who had been a successful interiors photographer, the farm naturally gave rise to an antiques business. Colt Barn Antiques, operated in one of the farm's early barns, is a well-trafficked haunt for collectors of vintage Americana.

The farmhouse itself may explain the two owners' activism in

Left: *Eclecticism prevails in the dining room, with early French chairs, an American cupboard, and folk art.*
Right: *The living room is a composite of antiques, including an 18th-century leather-and-inlay Korean coffee table.*
Below: *Celebrating its 200th anniversary as a breed, the Morgan is a gentle pleasure horse for saddle or harness.*

Left: *A framed collection of early 20th-century seed packages decorates a bedroom.*
Right: *Thin-necked antique bottles add interest to an 18th-century Italian table in the bedroom's adjoining sitting room.*
Below: *A farm dog patrols the public road that divides the barn from the house—an early New England building concept.*

preserving the past. About 200 years old, the structure is quintessential New England: a full Cape Cod that has been added onto over the centuries, "extending as the need for more space grew," says Howard.

"When we first saw it, it wasn't a matter of falling in love with it, but it was this deep sense of serenity that was overwhelming," he says.

That made decorating the home relatively easy. No special schemes, no out-to-impress airs were required.

Furnishings they already owned, including some unlikely Oriental and august 18th-century French pieces, were used in the farmhouse for "quite a mix," admits Howard. "But in decorating, it's the relationship of objects more than the objects themselves that counts."

Some 2,000 public visitors go to the farm each year to see Richard's traditional Morgans—and still others to buy Howard's antiques.

Those activities keep the place dynamic year-round, but Richard says the farm's abiding attribute is something even more basic: "It's home," both to the owners, and to a horse named Morgan. □

PRACTICE MAKES *Perfect*

By Steve Cooper
Produced by Bonnie Maharam

When deciding on house design, Ron and Lori Lunn are drawn by the sense of history they feel in a saltbox home. They appreciate the flavor of its raked roofline. The way it preserves the past. Its appealing good taste.

So, after joyfully succumbing to a longtime desire to reside in Connecticut's gentle northwest

Above: *Ron and Lori Lunn's former saltbox in Princeton, Massachusetts.* Above top: *Their Connecticut house.* Far left: *Dinner guests find antique dining room doors a perfect match for a custom-crafted reproduction table.* Left: *Fresh flowers, an antique rocker, and a warm fire make the living room a comforting haven. The chimney breast was fashioned from salvaged panels.*

127

PRACTICE MAKES PERFECT
• • •

hill country, they nearly duplicated the New England saltbox they previously built 150 miles away in Massachusetts.

"It's a style we were comfortable with, and it's my desire that guests feel at ease and relaxed, no matter what their particular

taste may be . . . I take pleasure in creating an atmosphere of charm and warmth," Lori says.

With its mix of historic style and modern convenience, the Lunns' former residence was featured in the May/June 1984 issue of *Country Home®*. Their new saltbox retains the savor while adding some spice.

Like all things done well, the three-bedroom dwelling gives the impression it has been effortlessly fashioned. By applying what they learned from their previous home, the Lunns have shaped an even more authentic period look. Carefully chosen antique pieces, including early doors, hardware, countertops, and windowpanes, help create

Below: *The Lunns' prior residence was featured in* Country Home® *in 1984. Back then, Ron explained, "We wanted the warmth and charm of an early house and the convenience of a new one . . . a house with instant age."*

Far left: *A table dating to 1760 helps create the same sense of time in the Lunns' Connecticut house.* Above top: *The keeping-room view is enlived by a harvest of flowers.* Above left: *Plants bask in a room set aside for potting chores.* Left: *The keeping room is warmed by an 18th-century Count Rumford-design fireplace, with shallow firebox and slanting interior walls.*

PRACTICE
MAKES
PERFECT
• • •

comfortable surroundings that speak of the past.

"Our house is our hobby, and together we garden, stencil, cook, and select antiques and accents for the house. Each antique we have found together has created a warm memory and story for us," explains Lori, who makes home a full-time job.

The foundations of the two houses are identical. With the exception of the exterior stain, differences are subtle. The most striking change has been made in the kitchen, where vintage materials lend authenticity to the look. Modern appliances are hidden by cabinets and paneling made from 18th-century materials. But the Lunns sought to balance a desire for atmosphere with the practical, everyday needs of preparing meals.

"Wherever possible, we tried to cover up those things that might spoil the impression. But there are practical considerations. You try to be consistent with the atmosphere you're trying to create, but then there is the utilitarian side of things, too," says Ron, a salesman for a high-tech industry.

The final result is what counts.

"People walk in and they go, 'Wow. This is really a fun house.'

Below: *In Massachusetts the Lunns tried to fashion their kitchen to fit the spirit of their household. Although the look came close, modern countertops and painted cabinets couldn't quite capture the ever-so-illusory feeling of age the Lunns wanted. Ron says the kitchen is a challenging room to decorate because most time-saving appliances and materials have such a contemporary feel. The answer, as in other rooms, was to recycle old materials.*

Far left: *Cabinets and countertops are 18th-century materials sealed for easy care. Still, a stainless steel sink is a cooking necessity.* Above top: *A bowl of cinnamon sticks and pomegranates spices the kitchen.* Left: *Lori uses the buttery for display. Shelves showcase her stoneware and urns. The blue-and-white stoneware has both style and function.*

131

PRACTICE
MAKES
PERFECT
• • •

People respond to it," Ron says.

Lori adds, "We desired the ambience of an early house with the convenience a new house has to offer."

Another major difference between the old house and the new can be seen upstairs. Because the last of the Lunns' four children is now attending school away from home, they were able to eliminate an upstairs bedroom. They also paid more attention to second-floor detail, such as the use of salvaged doors and early hardware. Upper rooms are now among the first stops guests make when they are given a tour of the residence.

The couple credits antiques dealer Betty Urquhart of The Maynard House in Westborough, Massachusetts, and Fitchburg, Massachusetts, craftsman Jeff Dana with helping them orchestrate the home's mood. Ron calls Dana an artist.

In achieving their look, the couple paid close attention to details, such as beaded beams and 12 × 12 windows with imperfect antique glass. Also, more care was taken in giving pine flooring a look of age. But the Lunns also remembered this was a home, not a museum.

"We aren't purists. I look for things with eye appeal rather

Below: Another difference between the two houses is how bedrooms are decorated. Back in 1984, bedrooms weren't close enough to a period look for inclusion on visitors' tours. "We were still learning," Lori says. This room, belonging to then-9-year-old Allison Lunn, was the only bedroom photographed for the previous story. *Opposite:* The new master bedroom has come of age with a custom-built tiger maple four-poster.

Left: A downstairs guest bedroom has been added in Connecticut. The old pie safe is piled with quilts. *Above top:* A custom-made soapstone sink from Vermont rests in an early dry sink and helps give the guest bathroom a splashy atmosphere. Though perhaps impractical for everyday use, the stone basin is an appealing addition for overnight visitors.

Below: *Lori sat amid her flowers and herbs in Massachusetts. "My father is a good gardener. It's a joy to him, and he communicated that feeling to me when I was a child," she says. Above right: In their garden in Connecticut, Lori passes along the family tradition to daughter Allison.*

than for perfection," Lori says. Here again, Ron believes he is working with an artist.

"So many people have a collection of hearts or stoneware or baskets. But we've fit a wide variety into a very natural look and I give my wife's decorative skills credit," Ron says.

Bringing diverse elements together to shape her home is a source of great pleasure for Lori.

"I feel our house reflects our personalities, tastes, and interests. Our wish is that our home will bring pleasure to others," she says.

Like a painter contemplating

a subtle shadow here, a burst of color there, Lori selects each antique or plant with an eye toward the overall effect.

"But this isn't just about a house," Lori says. "Ron is my best friend and we truly enjoy each other's company. Each day we share together is a gift." □

Right: *The family's Connecticut backyard is an inviting park. Lori says, "I plant what I enjoy. We do the work ourselves and take pleasure in selecting the various herbs and perennials we use. Each month springs new color, blossoms, and texture." The Lunns added touches such as a 500-pound stone sink used as a bird-bath, a slate sundial, and teak benches. Mother Nature provides bright colors.*

October

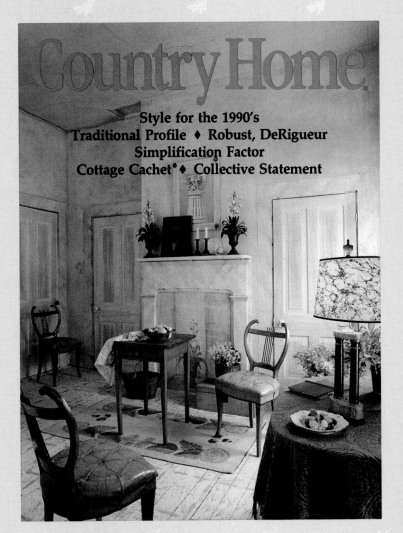

Country Home

Style for the 1990's
Traditional Profile ♦ Robust, DeRigueur
Simplification Factor
Cottage Cachet ♦ Collective Statement

SHOWCASE

Traditional Profile

Although as comfortable as last season's shoes, the traditional side of country gets new definition from the use of rich colors.

Traditional never looked so good as in this living room, where comfy upholstered pieces, *right*, easily combine with a few painted pieces such as the Austrian armoire, *above*. *Above right: In the dining room, a new table is paired with antique chairs. The table can be extended and pulled over to the Federal bench when guests call.*

Photographs: William Stites. Interior design: Thomas Burak. Produced with Joseph Boehm and Jean LemMon. Produced in conjunction with Drexel Heritage Furnishings Inc. Location: The National Christmas Tree Show, Washington, D.C. Furniture: Drexel's Country Collectibles collection, Drexel Heritage Furnishings Inc. Lighting: Frederick Cooper. Fabrics: Waverly.

136

Expectations were high when interior designer Thomas Burak set out to design two rooms for *Country Home* magazine. The assignment was to take a traditional setting (slightly formal, but a country staple) and infuse it with a new spirit. The result, shown here, includes all the necessary traits anticipated from a refined look and some that aren't.

Avoiding easy solutions that often lead to an inbred, expected appearance, Thomas mixed from a palette that contains not only paints but periods and finishes. For example, color used on the walls and woodwork, though rich, is muted with underlying tones of gray. This deviates from the crisp colors shown in the '80s—a reaction to the paints at Colonial Williamsburg being identified as more vivid than originally thought.

Inventive uses of antique accessories add a personal touch that only a collector can dictate: The drawing above the living-room fireplace, *opposite,* is actually the fire screen; a painting between the dining room windows, *opposite,* is an 18th-century roller blind; and the server separating the two rooms, *above,* is a country Sheraton drop-leaf table.

High-profile painted pieces—an Austrian armoire that could hide a stereo, a chest that doubles as a coffee table, and a Federal bench that supplies seating for dinner— cooperate with newer pieces to make the spaces more gracious. No compromise intended; these pieces weren't meant to do what they're doing, but they're doing it well. □

Strong color dominates the dining room, above, *where furniture in a warm nutmeg finish blends with an assemblage of fine country antiques.*

ROBUST, DE RIGUEUR

The face of country has changed dramatically in the past decade, but the style is as strong as ever. The four distinct looks that follow represent our prediction of country for the '90s. First, Southern European meets regional American in a new style shown in Tom and Mary Anne Thomson's home on the Mississippi River.

Houses, like children, are meant to be heard, not just seen.

Based on appearances only, the old half-stone home in Clarksville, Missouri, wouldn't have wowed anyone. Moldering and decrepit, it was an overripe candidate for the wrecker's ball. Rumbles around town indicated the circa-1820 structure would be razed to make space for a new city parking lot, with most folks prepared for good riddance instead of good-byes.

But that was before anyone allowed the house to speak.

Visiting the property in search of a vacation getaway not too far from their home in St. Louis, Mary Anne, a *Country Home®* regional

Photographs: William N. Hopkins, Hopkins Associates
Produced by Mary Anne Thomson with Bruce Burstert

editor, and Tom, an architect, were good listeners. They withheld judgment until the lackluster house could plead its own case.

Good thing, too: The couple immediately was arrested by the home's venerable voice—how it crackled with the livelier possibilities of the past, whispered its mysteries.

What Tom and Mary Anne heard within those peeling walls weren't the expected echoes of dignity and faded glory often incumbent with an old home. Instead, they discerned a dialect that was a strange blend of Huck Finn and Mediterranean basin.

They heard it in the primitive plastered walls, thick window wells, and a certain quality of light. Perched on a hillside overlooking the Mississippi

River, the house seemed to reverberate with picaresque lore—tales earthy, robust, folksy. And at the same time, the salty vernacular was tempered by a more lyrical inflection suggestive of sun-stained Greece or Italy or perhaps even the Provence region of France.

Of course, what the Thomsons ultimately heard was their own imaginations.

"With the river and the wonderful primitive quality of the home, we felt we could be anywhere. I love European country, and this house allowed me to have a sense of that," says Mary Anne.

That sense was strengthened by other, very real, sounds. The tinny, gay strains of calliope music threaded up the promontory from one of the river's majestic steamboats. And in hushed undertones, languorous breezes hummed through the home's many windows. The effect was surreal, neatly disposing of time and place.

Like Mary Anne, Tom wasn't unaware of the home's metaphysical dimensions. "In addition to its stately presence on a hillside, the house possessed a foggy aura of the past," he says.

And that was something the Thomsons did not want to lose after buying the home. Mary Anne soon had a solution.

Opposite: The table legs' chunky proportions and the chairs' rush seats convey a hearty southern European mood. Decorator/faux finish artist Bruce Burstert chipped walls of peeling plaster, then did a rag rolling over what remained for an antiquated effect. Below: A Biedermeier chair and drawings of classical architecture by Tom's father add a formal tone to the living room. But a hooked rug, simple linen swags, and a stenciled floor preserve the idea of casual country. All paint finishes are by Bruce.

The best way to make the house livable without silencing its vintage voice was to enlist the design and faux-finish skills of her friend, Bruce Burstert. A Kansas City, Missouri, decorator, Bruce had worked with Mary Anne on other *Country Home*®

feature houses, and she had faithfully followed his work ever since.

With his special knack for painting walls to look wonderful but weathered, and for furnishing rooms in timeless fashion, Bruce would be able "to leave a memory of the way the

house might've been, rather than to make it perfect," says Mary Anne.

In a bedroom, floors were stripped to reveal a hand-painted checkerboard pattern on the original wood planks. "I just painted a border around the floor and left it alone,"

FACES

says Bruce. "Then I painted the walls a very countrified faux paneling, with pale Naples yellow and a deep brick red."

At one end of the bedroom, where a door once existed, Bruce re-created a sense of the original room design by painting a faux door and bull's-eye windows.

Elsewhere, "the house had a lot of old plaster that we just kept. As I've done in the past, I worked with what was there and did my painted finishes over that," he adds.

A creamy glaze over pink paint festoons the living room walls, with woodwork and the mantel softly marbled in gray and antique white. The old pine floors, which had once been painted, were painted again by Bruce to reinstate the room's early feel.

The European country look is most pronounced in the dining room. "The walls were peeling plaster, so I chipped away at that and did a rag rolling over what was left," says Bruce. "This gave the room a wonderful, 'has been there a long time,' look. Even though the furnishings are American, the effect is more Provençal."

"Bruce's work allows you to feel how the house evolved over its lifetime," says Mary Anne. "It doesn't obliterate the past, but tells its story"—in the home's own voice. □
—By Candace Ord Manroe

Opposite: A hand-painted checkerboard pattern was discovered on the bedroom's original floor planks. Decorator Bruce Burstert, right, didn't alter the original paint, but called attention to it with the addition of a painted border. The roller-printed quilt is circa 1820. Ivy ball topiaries flank the mantel. Bruce's faux painting decorates a fire screen and masquerades on walls as bull's-eye windows.
Below: *The iron plant stand is by Darold Rinedollar, a renowned blacksmith who first showed the Thomsons the Clarksville home.*

SIMPLIFICATION
FACTOR
▼ ▼ ▼

Country comes clean in the '90s, integrating artful antiques with up-to-the-minute modernism—and all with a minimalist's touch. The vintage farmhouse of Michigan artist David McCall Johnston and family serves as a canvas for this study in reduction.

Top: *Artist David McCall Johnston and his wife and son, Ruth and Jordan, love Americana, as depicted in David's painting, "Fire Pumper to the Rescue."* Above: *Their circa-1840 farmhouse showcases American antiques such as the circa-1865 spatter-painted dollhouse in the entry,* opposite.

Photographs: Jim Hedrich, Hedrich-Blessing

Opposite: *A 19th-century general store counter is fitted with modern European fixtures in the kitchen; David's art tops a Shaker chair.*
Right: *A parsons table in the dining room serves as a foil for antique chairs. Also shown are an 18th-century wool winder, circa-1875 weather vane, Nez Percé corn husk bags, and a pre-Columbian pot.*
Below: *The parlor includes a circa-1848 Pennsylvania corner cupboard, a circa-1830 arrow-back settee, circa-1790 worktable, and Massachusetts box, circa 1828.*

The only superfluous item in the farmhouse may be an extra letter in the owner's name.

And even that is not without purpose.

David Johnson finds it professionally advantageous to paint under the more distinctive name of David McCall Johnston. The extra "t" doesn't disturb wife and son, Ruth and Jordan Johnson, though it does demand some explaining to new acquaintances.

Once beyond that minor inefficiency, however, the Johnsons' style is straight to the point: Home is crisp white interiors with pared-down appointments, all under the roof of meticulously restored circa-1840 architecture.

"We both like very stark white backgrounds," says Ruth. "Not a lot of clutter. We feel that antiques should be looked upon as works of art."

That stands to reason, as husband and wife each have an art background.

David is an acclaimed painter of Americana whose gouaches are included in numerous corporate collections.

Though Ruth has advanced degrees in education and has taught and owned her own school, she also weaves, studied art, worked as a metalsmith, and is now David's full-time rep.

Spartan, tightly edited spaces can be expected of artists. But the Johnsons throw a curve: They like their spaces minimal, yet they also happen to be consummate collectors of American country antiques.

Ruth and David have managed a pleasing merge of what sounds like two mutually exclusive predilections. Their antiques are carefully arranged in vignettes, with consideration to form, color, and texture.

A glance to any corner of the home reveals a kind of painterly serenity—a "real life" still life—that was precisely the owners' intention.

"I arrange [antiques] the same way that I compose a painting," David explains.

Even dining room chairs are selected for their sculptural quality. Each of the unmatched antiques "was bought because of its interesting silhouette," he says.

The clean country look is augmented by a few judicious dollops of contemporary design— sleek European lighting and kitchen and bath fixtures.

This unexpected blend of old and new, in fact, makes the home's seminal style statement.

"We both like American antiques, and I like modern [accents]. I pushed for the Italian lighting, which David also now likes because of its museum feeling," says Ruth.

For all their melding of antique and avant-garde, the Johnsons sacrificed none of the home's architectural integrity. They were awarded the house from the Farmington Historical Commission, based on their sensitive proposal for restoration. The couple disassembled and moved the structure to an acreage midway between Farmington and Franklin, then retained AIA architect Betty-Lee Sweatt for the restoration.

David's Americana art completes the home, mirroring the owners' interests. Says Ruth: "I tell people David not only paints Americana, we live it." □

—By Candace Ord Manroe

Below: *The master bedroom features a Shaker bed and hanging cupboard; a circa-1890 quilt made of printed flour sacks; and a Cape Cod spinning wheel,* opposite, *retaining its original paint. The chair and mirror are reproductions.*
Above: *A parlor vignette.*

COTTAGE
CACHET

Light and lacy, dolled up and doilied—so goes the standard lexicon of the country cottage. While this vocabulary remains viable into the '90s, its definitions will broaden, as the cottage is swept anew by unbridled imagination and a penchant for paint.

Photographs: William N. Hopkins, Hopkins Associates. Regional editor: Mary Anne Thomson

FACES

"Cachet" wasn't quite the term that came to mind when Joanne and Jim Evans first toured their pre-Civil War cottage in Elsah, Illinois. "Catchall" came closer to target.

"Polyester from 1970s' clothing was glued to cardboard and stuck on the walls. Pieces of Styrofoam patched the ceiling. Whatever was on hand at the time had been used. The colors were brown, black, and orange," recalls Joanne.

The couple bought the property anyway, inspired by its wonderful spaces for gardens and a hunch that, maybe, beneath the mishmash, lurked a comely cottage with erstwhile charms intact.

The gardens lived up to promise. But the Evanses' hunch about a buried gem proved good only as a case against following intuition.

"When we pulled down walls, nothing was there. That's when we just decided to use imagination and make it whimsical, for a cottage feel," Joanne explains.

Imagination is necessary for success in transforming any space, but unassisted, it can run amok. An essential handmaiden—the talisman that forestalls a sorry end—is talent.

A skilled artist, Joanne fortunately possessed both.

A trip to France—hours spent absorbing the beauty of Monet's water lilies—already had influenced her. Upon her return to the States, Joanne and her paint partner, Molly Phinny, soon were festooning furniture with impressionistic floral motifs.

When the Evanses moved into the cottage, after Jim accepted a position at the area

Preceding pages: Its living room cheery with Joanne's paintwork, the Elsah, Illinois, cottage is enjoyed by Joanne, Jim, and Ericka Evans. Opposite: Joanne painted floors and all furniture in the dining area and porch, above. Below: Entry "wallpaper" and "rug" are actually examples of the owner's artistry.

high school, Joanne had no compunction about her hand-painted pieces being perfect companions for the home.

The idea of using paint to create visual interest out of blandness spread. In Joanne's vision, every wall and floor of the home became a bare canvas awaiting her touch—skills with paint and brush that turned an ordinary cottage into a definitive style statement.

"Neither Jim nor Ericka [the couple's daughter] had strong feelings about this. But I did, and they were supportive," says Joanne.

Ericka's room was first on the redo agenda, for obvious reasons: "It had huge holes in the plaster and a gray-green moldy carpet. When Ericka first saw it, huge tears streamed down her face," Joanne remembers.

Using one of Ericka's favorite wallpaper samples as inspiration, Joanne hung a plumb line, eyeballed the space, and then freehanded her own striped pattern onto the walls using soft blue paint.

In the living room, guests are amazed at how closely a chintz pillow matches the floral "carpet"

Joanne painted on the wood floor. But the pillow preceded the paintwork. "I never try to duplicate fabrics, but I use them for inspiration. I want my work to retain some feeling of imperfection." Joanne is convinced her

hard work was not in vain.

"Every time I would begin to paint a wall or floor I would tell myself, 'Now remember, you're going to have to live with this, Joanne.' I think that's why it works." □

—**By Candace Ord Manroe**

Opposite: *Ericka's bedroom walls were painted by Joanne in pastel stripes crowned with garlands.*
Below: *One of her earliest creations, a trunk was enlivened by Joanne with swirling peach flowers; the box is more demurely patterned.*
Top: *Joanne painted the vanity.*

FACES
COLLECTIVE
STATEMENT

❖

The reign of cutesy clutter and homogenous collections draws to an end with the '80s. Country collecting's scepter passes to high-style hands, as announced by the eclectic Manhattan brownstone of Dr. Robert Bishop. In these unlikely urban digs, everything from folk art to Bakelite converges.

"Your daddy's got a barn, let's put on a show!"
Dr. Robert Bishop is convinced the kids in the old Mickey Rooney film had the right idea.

Long before the "Dr." preceded his name or he ascended to direct New York City's influential Museum of American Folk Art, Bob Bishop was a

feisty kid with a taste for quality and making a buck. His childhood almost eerily mirrors the celluloid yarn: *His* daddy had a barn, and the inevitable

Above: *Dr. Robert Bishop, director of the Museum of American Folk Art, is a consummate collector in his private life.*
Right: *His circa-1850 brownstone in the heart of Manhattan is an unlikely haven for his stellar pieces.*
Left: *Order is Bob's key to compiling collections. Gallery-style, his 20th-century American folk art paintings span an entire wall leading to the dining room.*

WILLIAM.L.HAWKINS 1

show was the first sign of the visionary spirit that would carry Bob as a central mover in high-level circles of art and antiques.

Bob's experiences as a precocious kid are important for another reason, too: They provide insight into the hows and whys behind the personal collection of American folk art that might well be a prototype for collectors nationwide in the 1990s. Bob's collection is that good, and his influence that great.

"I've always been a collector or involved in some way with the antiques world," he says modestly.

Growing up on a farm in Readfield, Maine, Bob developed his love for antiques from his grandmother, who was a

Left: *The living room contains late 17th-century New England armchairs, an early 20th-century icon, and a late 19th-century quilt.*
Middle right: *An old owl decoy that originally scared crows guards a new Tyndale lamp.*
Right: *Pewter ranges from new to 18th-century, a mixed-bag effect seen in other vignettes throughout,* top.

dealer. As a very young child, he loved to "work" at her shop—and can't remember a time he wasn't collecting. At just 13, he pondered those antiques already in his possession, stole a curious glance at his family's empty barn, and devised a plan.

In some ways, his scheme was even more ambitious than those in the movies: Bob envisioned not a one-time, rafter-raising event, but a permanent exhibition of

antiques that would be an ongoing source of revenue for the sole proprietor, who would never have to leave the farm.

Bob's irrepressible energy

and entrepreneurial know-how didn't stop at the farm, though. At 15, carrying as his most prized possession the unthinking self-confidence of youth, he came to New York City, got theater jobs working the Sid Caesar and Imogene Coca shows, and simultaneously opened his own antiques gallery. He went on to obtain a doctorate in American culture from the University of Michigan, write or coauthor 33 books (with more in the works), and serve as a curator of the Greenfield Village and Henry Ford Museum in Dearborn, Michigan.

Today, in addition to his professional ranking as the foremost authority on American folk art (he even instituted masters and Ph.D. degrees in Folk Art Studies at New York University, where he still

❧

Left: A reproduction of the original painted bed, also owned by Bob, enlivens the bedroom, with Phil "Chief" Willey folk paintings and a double wedding ring quilt.
Right: Two circa-1870 Shaker chairs define the bedroom's nautical nook.
Top: A fish decoy and folk carvings are intermixed.

serves as adjunct professor), he is a stellar collector in his private life. His Manhattan brownstone is filled with testaments to his life-long absorption, and the scope of these collections is vast.

"I have no one favorite collection," he says. "I love everything for itself. That's why there's such an extraordinary range here."

Brought together under one unexpectedly urban roof are a gallery's worth of new and old folk-art paintings, authentic

Shaker and Mission chairs, Bakelite radios, art deco and early-18th-century New England furnishings, naive religious carvings and rare decoys, and startling Amish and early-American quilts.

Interestingly, the effect of all this diversity is anything but cacophonous; instead, a soothing calm pervades the apartment, every object appearing harmoniously in tune with the others.

Part of this harmony can be explained by Bob's

eye—as intuitive as it is educated. He can sense when it's OK to juxtapose a hand-painted folk art bed with manufactured Bakelite radios; doesn't have to be told a 1920s Mission chair will work perfectly well just feet from an 18th-century table; needs no one's permission to flank Shaker chairs around a non-Shaker table that's really much earlier and, in fact, isn't technically a table at all but a convertible chair table.

This unerring eye for display and design also spares the apartment from the "too much" syndrome—a potential disaster that threatens every serious collector. The astonishing number of folk-art paintings in Bob's collection, for example, undoubtedly would be as confusing as clutter if scattered in groupings across every wall in his brownstone. But order is imposed—and the integrity of the individual works retained—when the

❧

Right: Shaker chairs flank a convertible chair table. A late 19th-century southern turtle quilt with raw cotton-ball batting hangs on the wall. Top: Bakelite radios rest atop an old Mt. Lebanon Shaker chest.

entire collection is hung, gallery-style, from ceiling to floor on the wide brick wall that sides the staircase and serves as an artful backdrop for the living room.

But something else is responsible for the home's lack of discordance. It still has to do with Bob's eye, but not so much in terms of room design or display as in how that eye goes about selecting each piece that comprises a collection.

The individual merits of every furnishing objet d'art in his apartment, no matter how superficially distanced in provenance or style, are weighted identically. The two inseparable criteria are quality and personal appeal—the head and the heart—with the eye speaking for both.

"The issue for me always is quality. Something need not be expensive to be of fine quality," he explains. "Oftentimes, just the opposite is true. What's important is that the collectible be distinctive, unusual, unique. Investment potential doesn't enter into it for me; for me, quality always assures that the piece is a good investment."

Bob defines the task of evaluating quality as intellectual. One measure of quality, for example, would be "how well a piece represents the social conditions of its period."

But a soulful as well as a mindful collector, Bob insists, "No matter how old a piece or how well it demonstrates the social and artistic tastes of that time, if it doesn't have a kind of character, it isn't very interesting to me. Everything I buy must

have a presence. I would never buy something as an investment if I didn't like it. I live with these things every day. They have to have some kind of meaning."

Bob believes if collecting is pursued with the intellect and emotions having separate but equal voice, designing a room or home to accommodate these collections is a snap: "You just put it all together, and it works." ☐

—By Candace Ord Manroe

December

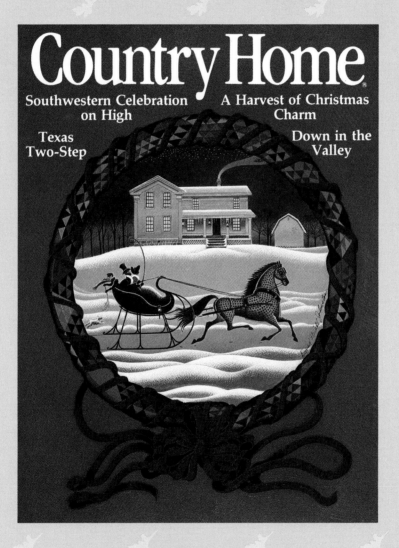

Country Home.

Southwestern Celebration on High   A Harvest of Christmas Charm

Texas Two-Step   Down in the Valley

Texas Two-Step

Fredericksburg couple adds antiquity to 1950s home—then re-creates the best of Christmas past.

By Candace Ord Manroe. Produced with Amy Muzzy Malin

Native Texans, in general, regard their birthplace as a point of pride. Those from the caliche-and-cactus swells in the central portion of the state known as the hill country are an exception only by degree: They seem to be just a little prouder, to put just a little more emphasis on the particulars of their birthright.

Charlene and Jack O'Neill consider themselves lucky to have been born in Texas, smart to have moved to the hill country. "It was a twenty-minute decision," says Charlene.

"We were on a weekend tour of the hill country, and Fredericksburg was the first stop. We never went any farther. The weekend was spent with a real estate agent, and we put our house in Fort Worth on the market first thing Monday morning," she explains.

Top: *Charlene and Jack O'Neill sell antiques from a small shop Jack built next door to their home,* above, *formerly a drab, 1950s asbestos-sided box.*
Opposite: *Jack paneled the living room in old cypress. The circa-1850 rocking horse features its original paint.*
Left: *Charlene's painting hangs above a 19th-century Amish blanket chest.*

Photographs: Rick Taylor

Texas Two-Step

Little wonder. With a stubble of bluebonnets across its craggy face, Fredericksburg is unquestionably handsome, if rugged. It also is something of a mecca for antiques lovers, who find its early *fachwerk* (half-timber and stone) houses ideal for displaying collections. Although Charlene and Jack sell and collect antiques, it wasn't one of the old German houses they chose.

Instead, in a nondescript 1950s box house, they saw what few others might: new additions for adequate space; applied antiquity in the form of hand-paneled walls, old floors, and beams and moldings—in short, the raw stuff of dreams.

Both are talented craftspersons, with good eyes for design. Between the two, they knew they could take the box and transform it into a convincing colonial-style showcase for antiques of that vintage. And because they would have put so much of themselves into the home by the time they were done, they knew that for special occasions, such as Christmas, no other place could have quite the same meaning.

They doubled the size of the house by adding a living room, master bedroom and bath, and a sun porch. "It's an ongoing nine-year project with more little touches to go," says Charlene. Surface compound and gypsum board were applied to the walls, which Charlene then stenciled.

Opposite: *The living room was added on by the O'Neills, with Jack installing old salvaged pine as flooring; he added chair-rail molding from a circa-1800 Pennsylvania log home. Charlene stenciled the room using a Moses Eaton pattern. The country Chippendale sofa is an old Vermont piece that was crafted from a rope bed. Above it are circa-1830 American primitive portraits still in their original frames; Jack built the reproduction tea table. An old two-piece Pennsylvania cupboard includes a pie shelf.*
Above: *A large 19th-century American rocking horse with original paint and tack guards a sun porch added by the O'Neills.*
Below: *A late-19th-century New England sled with original paint and iron swan-head runners dominates a kitchen table heaped with Charlene's favorite Christmas baked treats. Redware is displayed in a cupboard Jack built from old materials.*

167

Each old floorboard was laboriously installed by Jack, whose latest coup was to hand-panel the living room in the fashion of a colonial parlor.

When the couple bought the home, its exterior was outfitted in drab asbestos. Today, it boasts a bright coat of barn-red paint, a new tin roof for weathering hill country hailstorms, and a front porch that helps cut the harsh Texas sun.

Adjacent to the house, Jack built a shop for the couple's antiques business. The design is based on the German settlers' Sunday houses—one-room dwellings built by farmers and ranchers who went to town for church once a week and needed a place to stay overnight.

Jack came by his do-it-yourself skills honestly: His father was a woodworker and cabinetmaker. The few furnishings in the home that are not antiques were crafted by Jack, and all of the antiques that had been in disrepair were restored by him.

Charlene had an equally strong upbringing in her forte, antiques, growing up in a home where both parents collected. In addition, she paints naive art, is a renowned rug hooker, and restores antique dolls and toys—her special love that commands prime attention in the home at Christmas.

The combined talents of the couple result in nearly every inch of the home and its furnishings having

Opposite: *Made "old" by Jack's addition of wainscoting, beams, and wood floor, and Charlene's stenciling, the dining room is part of the original 1950s structure. Jack crafted the dining table from old cypress, fashioning the base after an 18th-century trestle. Flanking it are circa-1800 American Windsor chairs.*
Above: *Highlight of the room is a circa-1830 corner cupboard from Finley, Ohio. Using a heat gun, Jack spent three weeks removing six to eight layers of paint, saving 90 percent of the original coat, including a handpainted design on the drawers.*
Below: *Resting in an antique Vermont doll carriage is a circa-1845 German doll with papier-mâché head. The antique German feather tree is decorated with traditional German homemade cookies and antique glass ornaments.*

personal significance. Though they share an overall taste in antiques—informal 18th- and 19th-century American country—Jack and Charlene both have their favorites.

"My favorite American pieces come from the countryside surrounding Philadelphia, where the small-town cabinetmakers were influenced by the great formal Philadelphia furniture," says Charlene.

For Jack, the prize collectible is a black-glazed redware pitcher that measures more than a foot tall. "It is unusual to find large pieces intact because they have such a fragile composition," he says. "They were not fine pieces but everyday common ware that broke easily."

Like most collectors, the O'Neills anticipate Christmas as a time to display their seasonal antiques. Antique feather trees shelter old papier-mâché dolls and bear antique ornaments; an early white ironstone doll tea set is rendered appropriate as a cozy holiday vignette; a 19th-century rocking horse snuggles close to the living-room fireplace.

And year-round pieces—Pennsylvania cupboards filled with pewter or redware—become even more enticing when dressed in evergreen boughs and pinecones. Homemade treats are a final holiday touch, true to the personal spirit that permeates the home, all year long. □

Opposite: *An early-1800s pine chest bears original salmon paint and is home to antique German dolls and toys. The bed and oak-leaf quilt are 19th century.*
Below: *An addition, the master bedroom includes a bed with 1800s pencil posts and a headboard made by Jack. The covering is circa-1800 linsey-woolsey, one of the earliest forms of a quilt.*
Above: *Papier-mâché head dolls.*

SNOWY SECRETS

Down in the Valley

Two families
share the
snowy secrets
of Telluride,
Colorado, in the
shadow of
the Rockies.

By Candace Ord Manroe

During two months of winter, the San Miguel River Valley on the western edge of Telluride, Colorado, is untouched by sun. For a home hidden in the mountain's dark shadow, its lawn a tundra of drifts and ice, interior warmth means much more than a comfortable mercury level.

To Page and T. D. Smith and their young son, Alex, warmth means visual coziness—an imperative, not an option, for staving off winter's melancholic moods. And never is this need for a comfort-filled, beckoning refuge more important than at Christmas.

The thin whistling of a whiteout just beyond their windows doesn't chill the Smiths' spirits. They spend the holiday surrounded by the things they love—special rustic furnishings, a ceiling-tall live Christmas tree with old-fashioned ornaments, their log home, and the adobe-style architecture of a new living room addition. If anything, the outdoor activity only heightens the mood indoors, serving as a frigid foil for this holdout of warm holiday cheer.

Top: *T. D. and Page Smith and son Alex never fear a white Christmas in their cozy year-round home just west of Telluride,* opposite.

Left: *After Alex's birth, the Smiths hired architect Lynn Kircher to design a two-story addition on the front of the house, giving them a new living room whose architecture is compatible with that of the original.*

Above: *An antique and two locally crafted new spurs add to the room's southwestern ambience, along with an unusual small window.*

"Christmas is really a busy time because my husband and I both have businesses here," says Page. (T. D. is president of Telluride Real Estate Corporation, and Page co-owns a design shop, Interior Motives, in a historic building on Telluride's main street.) "But we try to make it special, starting our celebration Christmas Eve. We always have a nice dinner with friends here."

Page moved to the Telluride area 16 years ago. The back-to-nature movement of the '60s and early '70s was still exerting its tug, and she chose this corner of Colorado for its beauty, "sort of like a pioneer because the area was then so unsettled."

She hasn't lost that appreciation for nature. For the holidays, Page avoids anything smacking of the artificial and decorates only with natural greens plucked from trees just outside her door. Sweet-smelling pinecones fill baskets and bowls throughout the home.

With its human-scale proportions and appealing rough-edged architecture and furniture, the Smith home is a holiday haven with year-round appeal. □

Bottom right: A Colorado-crafted twig settee, built-in cabinet made by an area artisan, and an antique Portuguese milking stool set a simple, earthy mood for this section of the living room.
Above: The breakfast table is graced by a wintry view.
Top: The Smiths' cat, Z, snoozes on Alex's bed.
Far right: Originally the log home's living room, the antiques-filled dining room captures a sense of the seasons through rustic French doors.

Southwestern Celebration on High

Family trades Midwest for Southwest come Christmas

By Candace Ord Manroe

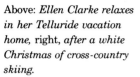

Above: Ellen Clarke relaxes in her Telluride vacation home, right, *after a white Christmas of cross-country skiing.*
Opposite: Lodgepole pine chairs and Indian pottery declare the living room's regional design. Because the home is passive solar, a stove is favored over a fireplace, which would draw heat out of the house.

Bread-and-butter realities have Chip and Ellen Clarke calling the Midwest home most of the year. But come Christmas, their holiday spirits are seasoned with a hearty dash of southwestern piquance. When the winter sky deposits soft powder on the slopes and peace in the air, the Clarkes head for their second home high atop the Colorado Rockies.

Avid skiers, the family had spent nearly a decade in search of the right resort property for a vacation home. "We wanted to be in a ski resort area, but we also wanted to be able to climb and fish and hunt. We wanted to have all of those activities in one spot and be able to use the home year-round," explains Ellen.

A ski trip to Telluride left them impressed. They enjoyed the Wild West history and savored schussing down the area's world-class slopes.

Opposite: *The dining room shares an octagon-shaped space with the living room—a design architect Robert Roloson hit upon after viewing Mexican tiles.* Below: *Pink and white lilies combine with southwestern elements—old Indian dolls and an antique Indian weaving used as a runner—to create an unusual centerpiece.* Above: *Ellen's antique pine hutch displays Italian pottery; the antler sconce is English.*

"We were awed by the beauty. It reminded us of Switzerland," says Ellen.

They returned in the summer and fall. Finally, on a mountaintop at a 9,000-foot altitude, with the kind of vistas that inspire silence more than poetry, the search ended.

To design a vacation home on this site, the Clarkes retained architect Robert Roloson, who already had a track record as the Clarkes' architect in the Midwest. Robert had no difficulty adapting to the new geography: The fact that he moved to Telluride as a year-round resident after only a few inspection trips for the Clarkes attests to his enthusiasm—and success—in building according to the site. A configuration of octagonal clusters around squares, the contemporary Alpine home that resulted is a natural.

"We wanted a house designed around the spectacular views, obviously, and we wanted a functional house that wasn't terribly large," says Ellen. A passive solar design, with its generous windows, accomplished both goals.

Thanks to that design, the Clarkes' first Christmas in the home (1988) had all the feel of being plopped into the middle of a scenic winter-wonderland postcard. The views of outdoors—breathtaking sweeps of snow-capped peak after peak—brought in through massive

Above: *Three shades of lavender on the walls and ceiling bathe the downstairs bedroom in color. The hues are echoed in Ralph Lauren fabric on the bed, and in the John Nieto painting—one of Ellen's favorite pieces.*
Right: *Chip and Ellen's son, Sheehan, a New York actor, relaxes in a second downstairs bedroom.*

windows in each room are as much a part of the interior as any furnishings.

With nature's vistas as competition, the interior required bold design to hold its own. Ellen called on designer Edana Westrich, who introduced audacious color—a rich palette of a dozen shades of pinks, roses, peaches, and lavenders—as the logical solution.

For Christmas, Ellen follows that color cue in determining her holiday decorating: "I decorate in mauves and pink, mostly with pink poinsettias." She also uses old American Indian dolls on tabletops for a slightly offbeat, distinctly regional look.

On Christmas Eve, presents are opened in the dining room after a traditional turkey dinner. That frees up Christmas Day for Mass—and cross-country skiing. Even during the holidays, the Clarkes find that their home's best feature remains outside its doors. □

A HARVEST
OF CHRISTMAS CHARM

Fabric Santas and miniature log homes are the rewards for two Maryland folk artists' imaginative labors.

By Steve Cooper
Produced by Eileen A. Deymier

When James Cramer bought an aging Maryland farmhouse in 1984, he knew he'd limit planting to a small garden. But he has reaped a bountiful crop nonetheless. Not in wheat or corn, but in folk-art Santas, which collectors appreciate for their rustic charm and inventiveness.

It's little surprise that one so talented at shaping small things could also display gifts when shaping something the size of his house. But just as he does with his carefully detailed Christmas figures,

James has given meticulous consideration to reconstruction of the farmhouse.

"When I first saw the property, I knew this would be a perfect place to live. There was room for us, room for guests to stay, and room for work," says James, who owns the farmhouse with business partner Dean Johnson.

James has taken what was once an attic as his studio and spends most days there piecing together the bodies, beards, and clothes of his distinctive Santas. His

Above: *Like an elf preparing for the big day, folk artist James Cramer adds distinctive detail to another of his Santas as the holidays approach. He takes great care to craft each figure individually. "I don't want them to be mass-produced and lose their personality. I want to keep them the original characters they've always been," he says.*

Right: *Some woodworking features suggest this Keedysville, Maryland, farmhouse may date to the late 1700s. It is both home and studio for James and business partner Dean Johnson.*

Above: *This was the first Santa fashioned by James. He says, "I can't bear to sell it." The log schoolhouse comes from Dean's collection of miniature structures made from general store crates.*

Photographs: William Stites.

181

portfolio of rich creations would fill a sleigh with limited-edition St. Nicks, delicate angels, and other Christmas figures.

Although it's easy enough to find generic Santas, James steers clear of visual clichés. Instead of a jolly fat man in a red suit, those who buy a James Cramer Claus

Above: *The parlor cupboard is home to one of James' Santas and his collection of carved sheep made by German families between 1890 and 1910.*

may get Santa-as-shepherd or a southwestern Santa wrapped in a doll-size Indian blanket.

"I started this because I was tired of seeing so many Victorian Santas. They all look the same. For a house like mine, you need something else, a folksy look," James says.

His farmhouse is as distant from the refined whimsy of Victoriana as the North Pole is from the South. Its boxy practicality

knows nothing of gingerbread doodads. It was designed by a no-frills kind of people who toiled with their hands and valued a job well done.

James and Dean bought the farm after years of renting. They were weary from a cycle of renting a place, fixing it up, renting another, and going through the decorating process again. With its outbuildings and log structure, the farm was prime pickings for the pair.

It's located in rural Keedysville, Maryland. Recently, the community of 500 has been discovered by harried workers from Washington, D.C., who are looking for serene countryside within an hour's drive.

James, who was raised in a nearby village, knew Keedysville might have what he

Far left: *Entering the farmhouse, this small parlor is to the right. The red-and-white-checked fabric love seat is the only upholstered piece in the house.* Left: *An old West Virginia cupboard, stocked with James' collection of carved European sheep, is the parlor's focal point. The sled atop the open cupboard is inscribed "1906 MSK," and some young artist's painting of a horse, fence, and barn can still be seen on the wintertime flyer. Was MSK the artist?*

Above: *An Indian blanket protects this 1989-edition Santa. He carries a thimble-size birdhouse. James also made the oilcloth blackbirds.*

wanted—old log buildings. But he didn't realize how much history would come in the bargain.

"We still haven't traced the house back as far as it can go," he says.

They do know the house dates to at least the 1830s, and it is one of the original farmhouses in the area. They also found it was pressed into service as a Civil War hospital.

"We're not far from Antietam, where one of the war's bloodiest battles was fought. In the smokehouse out back, Dean found a powder keg lid. Apparently, when the fighting ended a lot of scraps were left behind. Things like wooden lids were later used by farmers to patch holes on barns," James says.

Likewise, the home itself was something of a patchwork. Recent residents made unfortunate attempts to modernize rooms with carpets, linoleum, and wallpaper. That seems a bit like wearing loud clothes in a cathedral. Some may do it, but it violates the atmosphere. Still, the men looked beyond cosmetics and recognized something special.

"I liked the feeling of the rooms and was so anxious to live here, I planted the garden before we even moved in," James says.

Like archaeologists, they peeled away the present and the near past to get down to the

Left: *James and Dean ripped away the kitchen's ceiling, carpeting, cabinets, and fireplace brick while restoring the room's appearance.* Below: *Logs still show traces of a long-ago whitewash.*

Above: *Though James' Santas may be similar, no two are exactly alike. This St. Nick and an angel in an Indian blanket are in James' attic studio.*

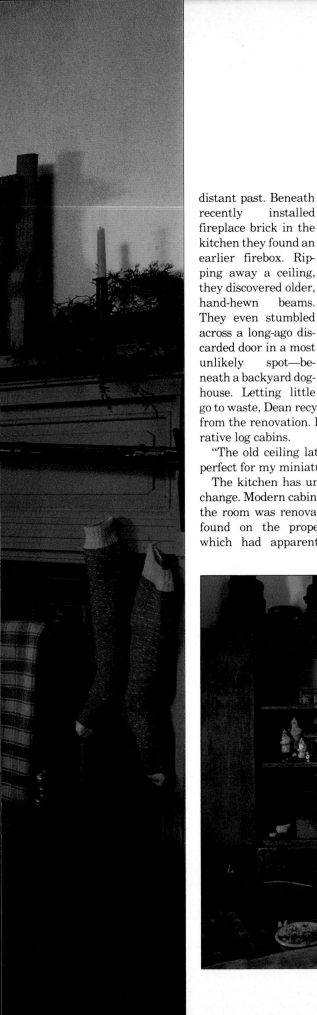

distant past. Beneath recently installed fireplace brick in the kitchen they found an earlier firebox. Ripping away a ceiling, they discovered older, hand-hewn beams. They even stumbled across a long-ago discarded door in a most unlikely spot—beneath a backyard doghouse. Letting little go to waste, Dean recycles cast-off materials from the renovation. He builds small, decorative log cabins.

"The old ceiling lath we took down was perfect for my miniatures," Dean says.

The kitchen has undergone the greatest change. Modern cabinets were removed and the room was renovated using old lumber found on the property. The bathroom, which had apparently been used as a mudroom before the advent of indoor plumbing, needed toilet and sink hookups.

"Most of the other rooms required replastering and scrubbing. When you start something like this, it always comes down to a lot of hard work," James says.

Almost all of the renovation was done by the two men. Unfortunately, a cracking and broken slate roof had to be torn off and replaced. So they hired a contractor to handle the elaborate job.

"I hated seeing the old roof go. But thirty-five or forty years ago someone covered that beautiful slate with shingles. The slate underneath was destroyed," James says.

From the massive renovation project, James came away convinced that no one

Far left: *A down-home feast fills the keeping room. It was prepared by Suzanne Worsham, a friend whose Virginia family home was featured in* Country Home® *in December 1987. On the mantel is one of Dean's cabins.*

Left: *Miniature cabins dating between 1890 and 1930 are kept in this Pennsylvania cupboard. "They were made as decorations to put under the Christmas tree and were made by fathers for their sons," James says.*

Above: *A chalkboard offering season's greetings and a copy of* The Night Before Christmas *help set the theme in this guest room corner treatment.*

Left: *The Christmas tree in this bedroom has patriotic flair with one of James' Santas waving Old Glory at the pinnacle. Sitting on the chest is a tall cabin with a blue tin roof crafted by Dean.*

Below: *James decorates with a light-handed simplicity using color and comfortably familiar elements. In this bedroom he gathers ordinary objects together for an extraordinarily livable effect.*

should consider such an undertaking until they've lived in a house at least a year.

"We really didn't do much the first year. Sort of put up with the way things were. But that year gave me time to live with the house and see which way things would work the best. By the time we started tearing out walls, I knew exactly what I wanted," he says.

The project also convinced him that a piece of conventional wisdom is wrong. Homeowners are often advised against residing in a house during any extensive remodeling. But James recommends staying.

"If you're willing to put up with the mess, it's much more practical to live in the house while you're doing the work. That way it's always staring you in the face. If you want to work all evening, it's right there to do and you're not as likely to put it off," he says.

There is no shortage of other work facing James and Dean. While James is a full-time crafter, Dean has only evenings and weekends to build miniature cabins. He still must work weekdays at a feed store, though he is hoping his folk art will soon become his sole occupation.

"Between the farmhouse and the number of art shows we've done in the last year, I think we've exhausted ourselves. I'm

Above: *Only three years ago, Dean took a few pieces of scrap wood left over from the renovation of the house and built his first birdhouse. Since then he has moved on to such complex structures as farmhouses, churches, Noah's ark, and a rugged miniature mill with a working waterwheel.*

Above: *One of Dean's more elaborate projects, this Noah's ark was specially commissioned. It took Dean less than 40 days and 40 nights to build it.*

putting in about seventy hours a week now on both my regular job and making my small log cabins," Dean says.

Where is such ambition born? Both Dean and James believe folk art is first and foremost a matter of the heart.

James says, "I've always been involved with art. I took classes in school. But I don't think you ever learn art. It's something that comes out of a person's heart."

For an example of this natural-talent theory, James can turn to Dean. For eight years, Dean collected lilliputian dwellings made from old general store crates. His admiration for the craftsmanship triggered his desire to become a folk artist himself three years ago. Now collectors seek out his downsize architecture.

"The most elaborate thing I've tried so far

was building a church. The doors opened up and you could see the choir inside," Dean says.

The choir loft was filled with James' fabric singers. Their next collaboration may be a Christmas scene with James supplying the Santa for one of Dean's structures.

Those who appreciate folk art agree with Holger Cahill, who organized a 1931 exhibit of folk sculpture for The Newark Museum in New Jersey. He said the folk school is an expression of the common people, not the idiom of an elitist cultured class. It is rooted in craft traditions and rare talents of gifted artists.

Whether applying themselves to their farmhouse or something the scale of a Santa or miniature cabin, there is nothing common about the work of James and Dean. It is both traditional and imaginative. □

Far right: *What bird wouldn't feel at home in this cabin crafted by Dean? The logs in the birdhouse are actually pieces of lath Dean collected after tearing out a ceiling in the farmhouse.*

Right: *Until recently, this shed was Dean's workshop. He left it for a garage that was easier to heat. "If your fingers are cold, hammering and nailing in January and February isn't much fun."*

Index

Page numbers in **bold** type refer to photographs or to illustrated text.

A–B

American rustic style, **58–63**
Antiques. *See particular type of piece*
Apartments, **14–23**
Aquariums, **14–15, 21**
Armoires, **136**
Balconies, **54**
Barn houses, **88–97, 98–106.**
    See also Log houses
Bathrooms, **39, 56, 133**
Bedrooms, **12, 13, 22–33, 62, 63, 97, 117,**
    142, 154, 160, 180, 188, 189
    guest, **56, 61, 78, 80, 105, 133**
    master, **38–39, 54, 55, 79, 85, 94, 95,**
    132–133, 149, 171
Beds
    Biedermeier, **23**
    four–poster, **30, 132–133**
    pencil–post, **171**
    rope, **22, 78**
    Shaker, **149**
    tester, **79**
Benches, **113, 134**
    Federal, **136**
    fire, **43**
    maple, **74**
    primitive, **61**
    settle, **43**
Birdbaths, **134**
Birdhouses, **190**
Bottles, antique, **125**
Breakfast rooms, **45, 75**
Breezeways, **92**
Brownstones, **156–162**
Butteries, **131**

C–D

Cabinets, **74, 85, 130–131, 174**
    apothecary, **25**
    corner, **77**
    kitchen, **27, 69, 93, 102**
Cape Cod houses, **118–125**
Capitals, **19**
Chair-rail molding, **166**

Chairs
    American arts and crafts, **18**
    arrow–back, **44**
    Biedermeier, **18, 141**
    French, **122**
    Hitchcock, **16**
    lodgepole pine, **177**
    New England, **158**
    potty, **46**
    rocking, **61, 77, 127**
    rush-seat, **140**
    Shaker, **147, 161, 162**
    wicker, **59**
    Windsor, **42, 53, 168–169**
Chaises, **116**
Chests, **82, 165, 170, 178**
Chimneys, **6**, 79
China, **43**
Chinese porcelain, **91**
Chintz, **110, 111**, 113
Chopping blocks, antique, **102**
Coffee grinders, **75**
Commode tables, **94**
Cooking tools, antique, **37**
Corn cribs, **121**
Cottages, **150–155**
Counters, **91, 147**, 102
    butcher block, **74**
    modern, **131**
Country French style, **90**
Coverlets, **79**
Cradles, **46**, 79
Crocks, **72**
Cupboards, **20, 21, 122, 183**
    chimney, **9**
    corner, **53, 66**, 83, **146, 169**
    Dutch, **9**
    hanging, **149**
    Pennsylvania, **166, 187**
Curtains, **18–19, 22–23**
Decoys, **43, 112, 159, 161**
Desks
    Adirondack, **62**
    mosaic-painted, **61**
    Pennsylvania pine, **12**
    plantation, **79**
    writing, **29**
Dining rooms, **26, 37, 44, 53, 60, 73, 92,**
    93, 103, 115, 122, 136, 146, 152,
    168–169, 174–175, 178–179
    art in, **156**
    combined with living room, **86**
Dolls and dollhouses, **42, 169–171**

Doors
    dining room, **126**
    French, **93, 94, 174–175**
    front, **33**
    passage, **35**
Doorstops, **61**
Drywall, **35**

E–K

Eclecticism, **67**
Fabrics, designer, **59–63**, 180
Family rooms, **76–77**
Fanlights, **18**
Farmhouses, **24–30, 47–56, 118–125,**
    144–149, 181–190
Faux finishes, **17–23, 140, 142, 153**
Fireboxes, **129**
Fireplaces, **34, 35**, 67, **84**
    in breakfast room, **75**
    corner, **87**
    Count Rumford design, **129**
    in family room, **76**
    kitchen, **10–11**
    paneled, **112**
    stone, **28, 54**
Fire screens, **136**
Floors and flooring, 27
    barn, **90**
    brick, **74**, 76
    painted, **142, 152**
    painted asphalt, **20**
    pine, **85, 166**
    stenciled, **141**
    stone, **92, 93**
    tongue-and-groove, **84**
Folk art, **54, 76, 122, 156–162, 181–190**
Furniture, primitive, 61
Garden rooms, **21**
Gardens. *See* Landscaping
Georgian homes, **6–13**
Glass
    doors in cabinets, **74**
    stained, **72**
Grain bins, **75**
Hallways, **48**
Hepplewhite tables, **115**
Homespun, **22, 74**
Hunt boards, **73, 76**
Hutches, **42–43, 178**
Indian art, **62, 69**